HOW TO BEAT
SCAMMERS

'If you think you're too smart to be scammed, think again. Nick has written an empowering, empathetic and essential toolkit for the fight against scams.'

Joe Lycett

'No one can match Nick's technical understanding of scams. This book is going to save people a lot of money and heartache.'

Matt Allwright

'Most people have encountered scams and think they're easy to spot, but with the huge variety of ways that scammers will attempt to steal money, it's essential to be aware of their tricks. *How to Beat Scammers* is a comprehensive guide to arming yourself against scams and even if the scam script changes, you'll be able to spot the important 'tells'. Essential reading for keeping yourself safe online and offline.'

Jim Browning

HOW TO BEAT
SCAMMERS

The Complete Guide to Keeping
Yourself Safe from Fraud

NICK STAPLETON

Michael O'Mara Books Limited

First published in Great Britain in 2025 by
Michael O'Mara Books Limited
9 Lion Yard
Tremadoc Road
London SW4 7NQ

If you or anyone you know has been affected by a scam, please see Chapter 10 for
a list of useful resources.

A CIP catalogue record for this book is available from the British Library.

This product is made of material from well-managed, FSC°-certified forests
and other controlled sources. The manufacturing processes conform to the
environmental regulations of the country of origin.

ISBN: 978-1-78929-755-3 in paperback print format
ISBN: 978-1-78929-770-6 in ebook format

1 2 3 4 5 6 7 8 9 10

Cover design by Natasha Le Coultre
Cover image credit Cam Harle
Designed and typeset by Claire Cater
Printed and bound by CPI Group (UK) Ltd, Croydon, CR0 4YY

www.mombooks.com

MIX
Paper | Supporting
responsible forestry
FSC
www.fsc.org   FSC° C171272

This book is dedicated to my wife, Lise, whose idea it was and without whom none of what I do would be possible, and to my mum, Lynn, for inspiring me to use my working life to help others.

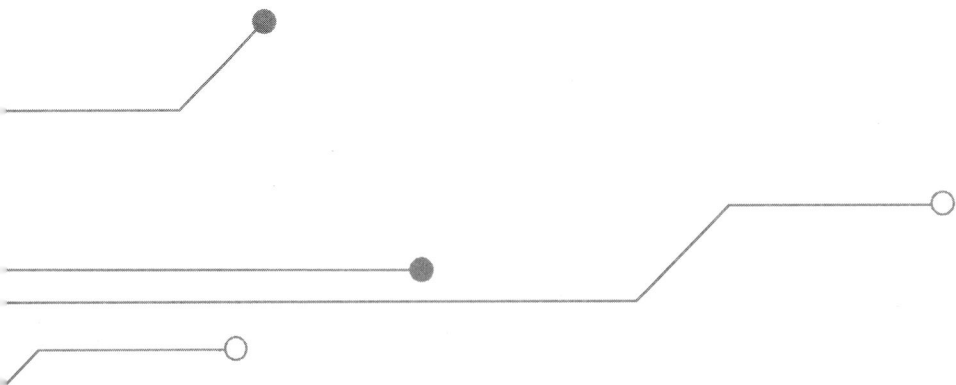

Contents

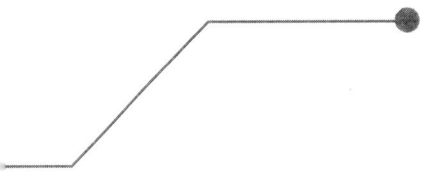

Acknowledgements

I wouldn't have been able to write this book without the guidance, input, love and support of the people below.

First and foremost my dad, John, who has always been there for me and provided amazing opportunities for me in life. The same goes for my mum. I watched her doorstepping people growing up and thought it was the bravest thing I'd ever seen. She never stopped wanting to help people.

My wife, Lise, for giving me the idea (she comes up with all my best ones) and providing the endless love which keeps me afloat. None of what I do is possible without her.

Without the guidance and mentoring of Matt Allwright, I may never have got into investigative journalism at all. It was conversations with him while making a show called *Housing Enforcers* together in 2013 that led me to a job on *Rogue Traders*, which had always been a bit of a dream for me. Working with Matt is always a pleasure, and I couldn't have asked for a better person to lead me into the world of secret filming and investigation.

The same goes for Rowland Stone, the TV executive behind *Scam Interceptors*, who I had worked with on *Rogue Traders* for some years prior. He wanted someone he could trust to go on camera and do a unique new job, with all kinds of ethical problems around our access and ethical hacking which hadn't really been faced on TV before. Very luckily for me, I fit that bill. Thank you to the whole *Scam Interceptors* team. Working with you is the greatest pleasure of my professional life and our work together absolutely inspired this book.

Foreword

You wouldn't believe how easy it is to trick someone.

I should know, because it's what I've spent most of my career doing, working undercover in the world of scams, fraud and the companies who are created for the sole purpose of trying to steal your money. Most of us take at face value the person we see in front of us, the website, the phone call, the text message or the letter we receive in the post. It is human nature to see the good in people and things and to assume that they, or it, do not have bad intentions. But unfortunately for us, that just isn't true.

I have spent thousands of hours of my life fooling people by pretending to be somebody else, more often than not wearing a hidden camera, putting on an accent, telling a story about who I am based on lies and deception. I have never once been caught. That isn't because I'm particularly good at it, rather it is because fooling people is fundamentally easy.

The story of the scam is almost as old as human history itself, traceable back as far as 300 BC, when two Athenian merchants attempted to commit insurance fraud on their own ship. Greek sea merchants Hegestratos and Zenosthemis are probably the first documented scammers, coming up with a plan to make themselves rich by taking out what was known at the time as a 'bottomry', essentially insurance money fronted as cover for their ship and its contents.

The agreement stated that after selling their cargo of corn, they would need to repay the loaned money with interest to the lender who made the agreement. If they failed to repay, the lender would take ownership

< 10 >

of their boat and everything in it. So Hegestratos and Zenosthemis took the ship out to sea completely empty and sank it, planning to pocket the loan and sell their grain on to someone else. It didn't work – Hegestratos died while trying to get away from the wreck, and Zenosthemis was apprehended and tried in the Athenian courts.

The progress of crime by deception can be followed right the way through history. Perkin Warbeck's attempts to deceive European royals in the 1400s into believing he was one of the 'Princes in the Tower' and the rightful heir to the throne of Edward IV was arguably the first ever publicized case of identity theft. Henry VII, the actual king at the time, didn't take too kindly to his claims and somewhat ironically had him imprisoned in the Tower of London as part of a wider conspiracy to usurp the throne. Warbeck was eventually hanged at Tyburn in November 1499.

François and Joseph Blanc's first telecommunications fraud was committed on the Bordeaux Stock Exchange in the 1830s after they bribed members of the optical telegraph system used to send communications from Paris to Bordeaux. At the time, the near 500-mile journey would have taken a week, meaning the faster you could get information from the capital's main stock exchange, the faster you could make money. Optical telegraphing was only meant for use by the government at the time, but it could send messages across the country in minutes. The Blancs made a fortune by bribing officials to send them coded messages using the system and were only caught two years later. They were put on trial in Paris but not convicted, as at that point no law in France covered the misuse of a telecoms network for personal gain.

There can be no more infamous example than the 1920s con artist Charles Ponzi, after whom pyramid investment schemes – where new investment money is used to pay original investors, creating an endlessly snowballing fraud scheme – are now named. By the late '90s, Nick Leeson was collapsing the UK's oldest investment bank, Barings, by covering up his own illicit and dangerous trading, made easy by lack of regulation in the financial sector. More recently, financier Bernie Madoff defrauded hundreds of thousands from investors in the US with a $65 billion take on a Ponzi scheme, the largest fraud by a single individual in recorded history.

As you track this murky history to the present, the amounts that fraudsters are capable of stealing seem to keep getting bigger and bigger. This is in no small part because it has simply never been easier to steal someone's money by deception than it is today. My experiences working undercover in unscrupulous businesses for the BBC's *Rogue Traders*, and more recently peering into the inner workings of fraudulent call centres for the BBC series *Scam Interceptors*, have put me in a unique position. I now find myself as a kind of outlet for the stories of those who have been scammed, receiving at least five or ten messages a day from victims from all over the world. This, and the decade-plus I've spent investigating the people who do this crime for a living, has made it very clear to me that the modern age is their boom time.

Whether it's a door-to-door salesman working for a business selling bogus insulation, a text message from a single scammer impersonating your bank or a 200-employee-strong call centre posing as government agents requesting underpaid tax, the scammers and fraudsters of the 2020s are winning, day after day after day. When they win, it means we all lose. That conclusion led me to write this book. Much of the information around scams is either unobtainable, spread across too many different resources, or is too difficult to access or too complicated to understand. My knowledge makes me able to gather all of it into one place in a way that I hope absolutely anyone will be able to understand.

Through reading this book, not only will you be able to put together many of the strange and fascinating pieces of social and cultural history which created the scam industry as I know it today, but you'll also be far better protected against fraud and scam attempts of all stripes. Perhaps

< 12 >

the most important thing to remember when it comes to this dark and unique business is this: there is a scam out there for every single one of us. If you haven't been caught out yet, it's not because you're too clever but simply because you are lucky. Eventually, the right scam will get you on the wrong day.

I would hope that if you read this book from cover to cover, it will help form a protective layer, your suit of armour against the fraudsters. This is how it should be viewed – something which might just save you in your time of need. I want you to read it, digest it and use it. Keep it beside the phone, on your desk, next to your computer – wherever it is you feel you are most likely to end up at risk. Grab it for reference if you encounter anything which rings a bell. But please, don't let it make you complacent.

With this book you will certainly be in a much better position to keep your money where it belongs than you were before you started reading. Bear in mind also that every time one of us doesn't pay out, like any real company, the scammers get ever closer to failing entirely and needing to find another way of making money. If all of us can do that, and in doing so make the industry of fraud unworkable, we can beat the scammers.

Let's put them out of business!

< 13 >

Part One

NO BUSINESS LIKE SCAM BUSINESS

1

The Fraud Explosion

An attempt at scamming or fraud is one of a very small number of human experiences which are entirely universal. Ask anyone if they've had a scam call, or a text, or someone try to scam them face to face, and they will almost certainly say yes. It's the biggest business in the world that everyone has had dealings with but knows almost nothing about.

For a sense of quite how big the problem has become in the past decade, take the global value of cybercrime, which would only cover fraud and scams that take place using the internet: it has risen from $3 trillion in 2015 to an expected $10.5 trillion in 2025. That makes the cybercrime community the world's third largest economy behind the US and China. The Federal Bureau of Investigation (FBI) estimate that the global scam call business alone now affects three out of five consumers. In Britain, 2023 saw 73 per cent of us targeted by a scam of any kind and 19 million lose money to one. Fraud is the UK's most common type of crime by some distance. As for a total value in Britain – the reality is anyone's guess, but it could be as high as £17 billion annually, according to an independent piece of research in late 2023. That's about the same amount of money as the entire yearly policing budget of England and

< 17 >

Wales slipping out of the economy and into the black market, never to be seen again. And yet only 0.1 per cent of British victims of fraud ever see any kind of justice. The UK convicts one in every 1,000 cases where a victim approaches the police for assistance.

The question of how we reached the point where someone trying to scam you is almost as common as brushing your teeth before you go to bed is a complicated one but can undoubtedly be blamed at least in part on the internet. It gave fraudsters a way to contact potential victims that was cheaper, easier and more anonymous than had ever been possible previously.

There are several reasons why the internet has created this fraud epidemic, but the first and most obvious is the incredible level of anonymity it offers to those who want to try to steal your money remotely. Where previously a criminal might have had to learn to pickpocket, burgle your house or take risks by attempting to mug you in the street, now they can download a fraud bible from the internet (yes, they exist), learn a couple of quick scams, buy a cheap pay-as-you-go SIM card and start sending out scam texts.

The simple fact of the matter, which is reflected by those statistics on conviction rates, is that the likelihood of getting caught as a fraudster in 2024 is virtually nil. That makes this extremely lucrative crime also a pretty low-risk one, and that's a highly powerful cocktail for anyone with criminal intent. The difficulty of investigating fraud for the authorities is enormous, because following a paper trail of stolen money in the age of online banking, cryptocurrency, virtual private networks and the smoke and mirrors of the online world is nightmarish. As such, those with the power to do so, like the UK's National Crime Agency, or the FBI in the US, tend only to go after the biggest fish imaginable, putting the effort in to take down organized gangs netting hundreds of millions off a single crime. That is a huge problem in the minds of those who have been victims of scams and fraud. To a single person, losing a few hundred or

< 18 >

thousand to a scam can be a truly devastating, life-changing event. As such, their expectation is that the authorities will do everything they can to turn the world upside down chasing the culprit – unfortunately, the reality is that simply isn't possible. The sheer volume of frauds happening at that size makes it impossible for the authorities to investigate every individual's case.

The global fraud explosion has created a situation where we simply cannot expect that the authorities are going to be capable of looking after us any longer. Also key is the affordability of fraud. The rise of broadband internet has made fraud an incredibly cost-effective crime. We now live in an extremely connected world, where a person in another country can quickly and easily go online, download Skype, WhatsApp or any other perfectly legitimate VoIP (Voice over Internet Protocol, essentially a call that goes through the internet instead of a phone line) service and start calling internationally at very reasonable rates.

The low cost of international calls made in this way has meant that where previously telemarketers planning on scamming would have wanted to keep their overheads low, so only dialled locally or within their own country, now the entire world is your potential victim for a scam over the VoIP phone. All you need is commonality of language so you can socially engineer your victim into believing whatever it is you're saying. This too has become considerably easier thanks to the enormous changes in the way we live our lives resulting from the widespread use of smartphones.

All this only became possible with the rise of broadband internet. Where twenty years ago, if you wanted to make a bank transfer you would need to attend the branch in person or make a phone call, nowadays this can be done in less than a couple of minutes using the online banking app on your phone. Alongside the creation of digital personal finances has come a range of smartphone applications to further increase the speed and ease with which you can pay out money to those who request it. Developers have streamlined payment systems to allow your smartphone to remember your card's details, requiring only your face or a passcode to pay out unlimited sums for products bought online or through an app. The pace of that change has been unbelievable – the way that the smartphone has entirely changed the world and our lives only comparable to the invention of the car or having electricity in homes.

While there have undoubtedly been an enormous number of positives resulting from the way the internet has changed the world, when it comes to crime the results have mainly been disastrous. In the space of a matter of years, it has created multiple generations of people in possession of smartphones for whom, due to their lack of understanding of the norms of modern digital banking or the behaviour of the tech companies whose apps they download, these phones are essentially just a sophisticated tool for fraud. That's not to say it is only the elderly or those who did not grow up with digital finances who are at risk of being scammed. The young are better connected, more tech-savvy and more likely to be in competent control of multiple different types of digital finance. But with the right approach from a scammer, it is far quicker and easier to defraud someone in their twenties or thirties than someone in their eighties who might need to visit the bank in person. That has led to a situation where 16–34-year-olds in Britain now account for more than 50 per cent of all the country's scam victims – putting paid to the notion that scams are just something for grandparents to be worried about.

What all of this means is that there is now so much opportunity for scammers and fraudsters to steal money, and so many successfully doing it, that every day more and more ways of taking your money are being discovered and brought into use. Trying to keep track of current scams as a profession is extremely difficult (I would know!), such is the pace of the scam business.

This too is aided by the internet – because not only do the scammers

< 20 >

now have the ability to work remotely, anonymously, in touch with the whole planet as their potential victim and everyone susceptible to scams – they now have the ability to communicate with one another more easily too. The murkiest corners of the internet like the dark web (essentially unlisted internet sites accessible only using an encrypted internet browser), encrypted messaging apps and even encrypted smartphones all facilitate their ability to defraud us.

There are whole websites dedicated to the exchange and sale of scam-related products and software. Need a way to quickly spoof your phone number so it appears as something else? There's an app for that. Looking for a forum to discuss the most effective ways of using stolen card details? Google it. Want to buy hacked customer data, like usernames and passwords? The dark web has got you covered.

By way of a real example of just how easy it is to get set up running a scam in the 2020s, take the 'Hi Mum' text scam which swept the UK and US across 2022 and 2023. Also known as a friend-in-need scam, it essentially relies on the concern of worried parents to get quick payments, believing they are exchanging text messages with their child, who has lost their phone and got a new number.

The scammer socially engineers the parent into paying by starting with a message like 'Hi Mum, dropped my phone down the toilet, had to get my mate to buy me a new one. Text me on this new number …'

When the parent texts, the scammer quickly explains that the new phone means they're locked out of their online banking and need to repay their friend for the new phone. Bank details are quickly exchanged and the worried parent helps out their child within minutes. The scammer potentially takes payment in the high hundreds or low thousands for a few minutes' work.

To be able to run the scam you need only three things: a smartphone capable of sending out text messages, which can cost as little as £40–50; a pay-as-you-go SIM card with some credit on it to send the texts out,

< 21 >

say another £50 max; and a bank account to take payment into, which probably belongs to a friend or acquaintance who is being paid a small portion of the profits to let you use their account to launder your income.

You'll need to buy some data too, let's say 10,000 UK mobile numbers which are in active use. This can be found on the dark web or an encrypted messaging forum for under £100 as well. If you're a really clever 'Hi Mum' scammer, you might even want to refine your data a bit to make sure you aren't wasting credit texting people who aren't of child-bearing age or who aren't women. To do so you can invest another £5 in getting a profile picture downloader app, which you can easily find a link to by searching scammer forums online. Put your 10,000 numbers in and it will download whatever picture that number uses on their instant messaging app, collating all the numbers and pictures into a nice document for you. That way, you can sit there and comb through the photos until all you have left from your original 10,000 numbers you bought for less than £100 are 2,000 women in their forties, fifies and sixties, who might reasonably have children old enough to have their own smartphones and online banking.

For the princely (and probably overestimated) initial sum of less than £200, you can now run a 'Hi Mum' scam from your bedroom. If you're successful in getting a worried parent to pay out the cost of new smartphone even once, you'll be making a profit of about £800. A good 'Hi Mum' scammer will be running multiple cheap smartphones at the same time, pretending to be about five to ten different people's children and taking payment within ten minutes of sending the first batch of text messages out. A really good 'Hi Mum' scammer can make thousands of pounds a day this way and afford to take a new short-term let apartment every couple of weeks, constantly moving to make tracking them down even more difficult. A 'Hi Mum' gang of five or six individuals working from multiple different locations could clear tens of thousands.

That maths is pretty scary. When the risk is so low and the profits so

< 22 >

high, it's not difficult to see why this type of crime appeals so much to those who do it. It is also an inescapable truth of the modern fraud landscape that the US and UK are targeted more than almost anywhere else on earth – this is borne out in hard statistics of fraud losses documented by NASDAQ's Annual Financial Crime Report. Britain has a far worse problem with scams and fraud than any other European country, despite having a considerably smaller population than Germany and being roughly half the size of France. The US, meanwhile, loses more to fraud annually than the entirety of the Asia–Pacific region put together.

There are a number of reasons why this may be the case, including the most obvious – language. The widespread use of English as the language of international trade and business has led to many, if not most countries around the world insisting it be taught in schools from an early age. The ability to speak the language of your victim has certainly always been a necessity when it comes to running a scam. Unfortunately, the US and UK's positions as the largest English-speaking countries on the planet with the largest pools of possible victims have likely made both disproportionately targeted by fraudsters.

Britain has gone further to make itself an attractive option by government decisions made over the past twenty to thirty years regarding trade, regulation and business. It is, without a shadow of doubt, the most attractive country in the world in which to launder money – a process necessary to any criminal looking to hide their ill-gotten gains from the prying eyes of anyone watching. As Oliver Bullough wrote in his brilliant 2019 *Guardian* article 'How Britain can help you get away with stealing millions: a five-step guide', when it comes to the act of stealing money, 'Britain is your best friend.'

Why? With the notion of making our country the easiest place in the world to set up a business, we decided to make it the easiest place in the world to do fraud. Until the introduction of the Economic Crime and Corporate Transparency Act in March 2024, you could set up a

< 23 >

limited company in Britain, registered with Companies House, our database of all listed companies in the UK and their directors, without submitting any form of identification.

Yes, you did read that correctly. Any criminal, from anywhere on earth, could make up a name, pay for a random PO box somewhere in the UK to receive post and start a limited company to launder money through. If you wanted a fancy address, you could pay 29 Harley Street in Central London to allow you to use theirs – 2,000+ other companies already do. The register of businesses at Companies House still has directors like Adolf Tooth Fairy Hitler and my personal favourites, XXXXX YYYYYYYYY and Mmmmmm Mmmmmmmmm. A multitude of babies are also company directors. Thankfully, this is in theory no longer possible with new registrations, as Companies House has, as of March 2024, finally been given new powers to at least check that the people registering as running businesses in the UK aren't dead dictators or noises you make while eating or fresh out of the womb. That said, with up to 5,000 companies sometimes registered in a single day in Britain, don't envy those with the task of checking out who's behind them.

If you're a criminal with the real intent of effectively hiding money in the UK's fraud epidemic, why would you even bother lying? You can just steal someone else's identity document to set up a company in their name, using their address as the office, and send all the documentation to them. You can run all the finances digitally anyway, so you don't need to worry about collecting your post.

The person whose identity you've stolen, who actually owns the property, will be worried, though, especially when they start receiving letters from debt collectors against business loans you have taken out in their name, or legal letters from lawyers representing your scam victims. And by the way, the onus is on them to prove to Companies House that they have nothing to do with your scam business by filling out a

< 24 >

tremendously complicated RP07 Dispute a Registered Address form. All in all, a great system.

By way of an example of how completely and utterly out of control the situation has become, Graham Barrow, a Companies House expert, documented that on 30 April 2024 (more than a month after the UK government finally reformed the system to include ID checks), almost 5,000 companies were registered in the UK in less than twenty-four hours. Out of that number, 647 were registered by Chinese nationals. That is not by any means to say that all 647 of these Chinese company directors are fraudsters, or that any of them are. It is simply a demonstration of the scale of the task we face in attempting to regulate this process.

I hope by this point you can see what I'm getting at. The combination of these many factors has created a situation where fraud is not now solely being perpetrated by individuals, or small groups in dark basements sat in front of laptops. As you will read in the next chapter, it has become big business.

When you look at the whole picture in this way, it's not difficult to understand why fraud has become one of the planet's most popular types of crime. Unless we collectively start taking major steps to protect ourselves and slow down the constant flow of stolen money, it isn't going anywhere either.

< 25 >

2

The Scam Map
of the World

The modern industry behind scams and fraud has tentacles sprawling all over the world. Different regions of our planet have developed their own specialisms, which in turn have developed into cultural phenomena in certain countries.

The next time you see that image of a hooded, slightly evil-looking man sat hunched over a laptop, pause and consider that the world of scams has moved on. It is no longer you against another individual with ill-intent; it is you against an entire ecosystem of like-minded people, many of whom see it as their 9–5 job. Suddenly the need to tool yourself up to fight back against this might seem considerably more urgent.

⊕ INDIA – THE SILICON VALLEY OF SCAM CALLS

India is the undoubted global headquarters of the scam call business, estimated by the FBI to be the source of 85 per cent of the world's fraudulent phone calls. These days, they are all run through the internet using VoIP, which massively reduces the overhead costs of the criminal syndicates making the calls.

For a quick potted history of exactly how India came to be this scam call monolith, somewhat confusingly we need to begin in Birmingham in 1965. The very first office we would traditionally know as a 'call centre' belonged to the Birmingham Press and Mail Building, dealing with business-to-business conversations for its clients.

By the 1970s, this approach had been adopted by banks like Barclays to help deal with customer enquiries, and so the modern call centre was born. By the 1990s, several big Western businesses had realized the opportunity existed to find cheaper alternatives to paying huge numbers of British staff to run their customer support – and the BPO, or Business Process Outsourcing, industry began to take shape. It is that which much of India's legitimate technology industry thrives upon today.

Seeking a country with a large population of graduates who had good IT proficiency and an excellent command of English, who would be willing to do the same work for much lower wages, over the next decade a number of companies (including Lloyds TSB, British Airways, National Rail and Tesco) struck on India as the new home of their call centres. The savings were enormous, as much as 40 per cent, despite the centres being halfway across the world.

Various Indian entrepreneurs saw the chance to set up shop, even giving their employees lessons in British celebrity gossip, making them watch episodes of *The Bill* and training them in English football's vagaries to give them the edge in dealing with British customers with maximum familiarity.

By the late 2000s and into the 2010s, it was becoming clear that the Western public were not in love with this new arrangement, and single businesses that had provided thousands of jobs in India started to pull out. Suddenly, the idea of their call centres being located in the Western world, or 'home-based', was a plus point in advertising campaigns. The script had been flipped.

One theory is that this change of heart created an opportunity for

< 28 >

criminals to step in. When the legitimate businesses began to pull out, three things happened. The first was that a huge amount of actual data on Western customers was left behind, in an era before GDPR, or General Data Protection Regulations, when we didn't have any kind of serious regulation about how our data should be stored correctly, or punishment for those who didn't follow the rules.

The second was that a good number of the many thousands of Indian call centre staff found themselves without jobs to go to. From the floor to the managers, they had been trained in how to do a very particular job, for which they no longer had an outlet. Crucially, however, the third, and more intangible, thing had already occurred. The idea had been created in the mind of the Western consumer that a call coming from South Asia related to customer support from a major company might well be legitimate. And so the Indian scam call centre was born.

For some of the same reasons that India was an attractive place to take customer support in the '90s if you were a Western business, now it is a very attractive place to run a scam call centre. More often than not, today's scam callers in India are employees of public-facing corporations with listed directors, some with hundreds of employees, human resources departments, real payrolls and their own IT people. Some of them are capable of making hundreds of thousands of 'robocalls' to the US, UK and Australia in a single day, provided they have enough data (telephone numbers) to support that volume of calls.

The robocalls themselves are perhaps one of the major gamechangers that led to the situation as it is. They are the carpet bombing of the fraud business, a tool allowing a single call centre to make contact with thousands of potential victims in a day, teeing them up for a scam with a single threatening robotic message without the need to employ thousands of people to make the calls. A classic is from the bank impersonation scam: 'Suspicious transactions on your debit card. Press "1" to speak to the security department.'

< 29 >

This generic type of message can be heard as soon as the call is answered and is frightening enough to get large numbers of people to do as it asks. If even 1 per cent of the 100,000 calls made in a day are put through, that's still 1,000 potential victims on the phone with your scammers. So at the first stage, you probably only need twenty-five to thirty people working as call receivers. These receivers simply sit and wait for fresh 'hot leads' (sales talk for an interested customer, in this case a worried potential victim) and start taking details from those who have pressed 1, before passing them on to a more experienced 'closer' to finalize the scam and take payment.

If just ten of the original 1,000 who pressed 1 are then turned into successful scams by a closer, with average losses to Indian call centre scams in the US mapped at $35,000 by the FBI in 2022, you can potentially turn over $350,000 in a day. With this in mind, a basic call centre set up in India might cost you an initial investment of around $15,000 to create.

A run-of-the-mill Indian scam call operation works like this: you make your initial investment and get your office space, computers and employees on board. You buy an international VoIP dialling package from a phone company and pay an IT support company to set it all up for you. If you've got the knowledge yourself, you write a script for your employees to use. This will form the fundamental basis of your scam. If not, you buy one which already exists from one of the darker corners of the internet. Bank impersonation, compensation scam, refund scam, you choose … The script is what it says on the tin, a written description of what to say during phone calls.

New recruits begin talking to their 'customers' (read: victims) with the script on day one. It contains a selection of 'rebuttals' – essentially responses designed to close down the objections of the person you're speaking with. For example, if the victim were to ask how they know that they are speaking to their bank during a bank impersonation scam, the

< 30 >

rebuttal might be 'we're based at number XX, on YY street in London', which is the genuine address of the bank's headquarters.

The script will have the scammer tactics that are common in these calls (impression of urgency, isolation from sources of support etc.) built into it, meaning your employees don't even need to be particularly good at conning people to be successful. They just need to stick to the script.

If they get the hang of it, the new recruits will quickly learn what works: the social engineering skills and manipulations, the changes of intonation at just the right times to apply pressure or induce panic, and the need to remain calm and professional even when being questioned by a suspicious victim. This will then see them graduate to the position of closer – your most valuable employees, the ones who get the money over the line and into your account.

With a few managers in place to watch over the 'sales' team doing this work, making sure they aren't slacking or taking too long on their breaks, you are essentially good to go. Get big enough and maybe you'll need to start worrying about your own human resources department to keep track of all the commission your scammers are making – or an IT department of your own to control and keep track of your calls.

Bear in mind as well that the methods of making money as a scam call centre are not only limited to what you are able to steal from your victims. Every piece of data acquired has value too – so the employees are taught to operate just like a real call centre would. During the calls, every bit of banking information they get from you is recorded by them on their screen: sort code, account number, date of birth, address. They probably only started with a phone number, but by the time the call is over they know your inside leg measurement.

When they are complete, every call that's made or taken is classified, known as making the number which related to the call 'dispositioned'. Customer shouting down the line, telling you they know it's a scam and never to call again? Dispositioned as a DNC, or Do Not Call,

< 31 >

their number removed from your data set. Customer busy but possibly believing what you're saying? CB, or Call Back. Customer hook, line and sinker and sent over to a closer? SM, or Sale Made.

The final result of this dispositioning of data is that after a day of calling 100,000 numbers, your call centre might end up with a very valuable thing indeed. Known as a 'Sucker List', it's the gold dust of the scam call industry. With a well-put-together sucker list, you can turn your scam success hit rate from 1 per cent to 50 per cent, no problem at all.

When you consider all the banking information obtained in the course of a bank impersonation scam, combined with personal information such as your number, date of birth and address, our scam call centre has built a very good profile of you, the victim, by the time the call ends. So what do they do with their sucker list of profiles? Sell them on to the next group of scammers. That's why those who have once been victims of scams will find themselves inundated by others trying the same trick – they're on a sucker list.

This extraordinary amount of money being made has to go somewhere, and it does. The scam call centres of India have come to support a vast web of associated businesses and enterprises, with those who are supplying them data, renting them office space or selling them phone and text packages also ultimately profiting from defrauded 'customers' across the Western world.

There is no doubt that, including this wider network in the pay of the scam business, there must be millions of people in India whose daily bread ultimately results from scams. Were this entire business to end tomorrow, it seems likely there could be a noticeable knock on the country's GDP.

When it comes to profiting from scams, there are plenty of larger scale, legitimate international companies with questions to answer – like those who sell the software that provides the architecture of how scam calls are made.

< 32 >

Want to know how many of these kinds of operations there are in India, trying to call the Western world six days a week (they work Saturdays), fifty-two weeks a year? Honestly, no one really knows. Jim Browning – known to many as the godfather of the 'scam baiting' community, which creates awareness around scams online, and also as our ethical hacker on the BBC's *Scam Interceptors* – has personally mapped hundreds in the years he has been pursuing his online investigations into their activities. Making *Scam Interceptors*, there has never been a day when we've been unable to listen to a scam call happening, despite only filming nine weeks of the year, eight hours a day for the past three years – and our access to the scam callers is only a drop in the ocean.

It is also hugely helpful to the Indian scam call business that a legitimate technology industry has sprung up in India in the past decade. As of 2024, it is expected to pass $250 billion in revenue, with a large part of that made up by Business Process Outsourcing. Even enterprises like Microsoft still rely entirely legitimately on BPO. Much like the call centre boom in the '90s, it means outsourcing parts of your business to skilled workers in a country where employing skilled workers is considerably cheaper than it is at home.

The result, however, is that within a tech hub like Kolkata's Sector V neighbourhood, or Gurugram outside Delhi, or Pune, Hyderabad and any number of other smaller towns and cities around the country, you will find scammers working in the same buildings as authentic operations. That's not to say legitimate tech businesses in India have any responsibility or part in the scam business – quite the opposite. The scammers themselves set up their own legitimate, public-facing operations that will be used to launder the money made by their scams, essentially hiding the stolen funds within the genuine work of the public-facing business. So, working alongside perfectly legitimate companies, in perfectly legitimate industrial estates, are seemingly legitimate companies that actually hide scammers within their legitimate operations.

< 33 >

Our investigations on *Scam Interceptors* have shown us this on multiple occasions – companies where, for example, work is being done on one side of the office in marketing for a genuine business, like questionnaire phone calls. On the other side of the room, however, there are twenty-five people pretending to work for Amazon's customer support and stealing thousands from every victim they get over the line. It makes the already complicated job of the authorities in trying to catch the scammers virtually impossible. Let's take the example of the journey of the money in the aforementioned bank impersonation scam, which is probably one of the most common used by Indian scam call centres.

An individual in the UK receives a phone call. The number calling shows as a local landline, so they answer it, believing it to be a local business or similar. It is our robocall, explaining that there have been fraudulent transactions on their account. If the victim is persuaded to go through with the scam, this is what happens to their money.

The UK victim uses online banking. They send money that day on the instruction of the scammer, by bank transfer, to another UK bank account. Bank transfers of cash in the UK are virtually instant. The money arrives in the account specified by the scammer, which will be controlled by a 'mule', essentially a co-operating person who is taking a small percentage of the income in return for the use of their account, usually 1–5 per cent.

The mule transfers the victim's money to another mule account, who takes their share. This second mule sends the money to a third account in the UK. All have been with different British banks. Finally, the third mule sends the money internationally to a bank in Latvia. That mule sends it to Thailand. The Thai mule finally sends the victim's cash back to an account in India, and it makes its way to the scammers.

The victim, in the UK at least, has likely lost something in the region of £1,000 to £10,000 due to the way our banking systems flag payments over £10,000. To them, a potentially life-changing amount but to the

< 34 >

police in the UK, realistically, not enough to be worth the trouble of even opening an investigation into where it went. And even if the police did – where would they begin? The paper trail of banks, following the money between multiple different UK institutions before leaving the country? This would involve co-operation with international law enforcement agencies elsewhere, so it's a huge undertaking.

Should they start with the phone number the Indian call centre used? It's a spoofed number, paid for, giving them the ability to appear like a local caller to the person who answered the call. The police could attempt to find out who sold the spoofed number by requesting data on the purchaser. But any even vaguely intelligent scammer would pay a third party to sort out their spoofed numbers for them, likely an Indian-based IT support company who specialize in call centre set-up. At which point the police would need to involve authorities in India to get the evidence necessary, meaning more international collaboration.

And even if the spoofed number data did lead somewhere, can the police follow it back to the scammers who originally made the call? How would they prove who made it? Most scam call centres use VPNs (Virtual Private Networks, essentially an internet connection which allows you to alter your internet protocol (IP) address, or your physical address in the world based on your connection), which means whatever IP address the authorities did obtain through the many layers behind the spoofed phone number would probably be wrong.

Ultimately, the prospect of any of this happening is virtually nil. There are extraordinarily few circumstances in which there has been justice for victims of Indian call centre scams in the past decade of British or US policing. If you attempt to search for examples online of recent efforts by UK law enforcement to collaborate with their Indian colleagues to shut down scam call centres, you'll likely find a single example from 2019. Because as far as I'm aware, that's the only time it's happened in recent years.

< 35 >

This demonstrates further how and why it is that the Indian scam call centre explosion has occurred – the chances of actually being caught, never mind prosecuted, for your role in stealing money from victims across the Western world is zero. Another key aspect of the scam call boom in India is that it is the most populous country in the world, with almost 1.5 billion inhabitants. This huge population leads to 12 million graduates joining the workforce every year. Despite having a relatively healthy economy in a number of areas, this is a rate that the country's skilled jobs market cannot support. Thousands of applicants may apply for single jobs in high skills industries like engineering. In 2022, 12 million applied for 35,000 railway jobs in one state, which resulted in riots for more positions to be made available by the employer.

In 2021, 85 per cent of the country's unemployed population were aged between twenty and twenty-nine – exactly the demographic of those most commonly working in scam call centres. In an economic climate such as this, it's not hard to see why the high commission potential of a job in a scam office like those we feature in our programmes appeals to a lot of young, English-speaking graduates for whom opportunities are not plentiful, despite their high level of education.

Here is where things get very complicated indeed from a moral perspective. It is difficult to judge the average Indian phone call scammer because 18.7 per cent of the country's population is vulnerable to extreme poverty. What this means in simple terms is that there is almost no social safety net in India; should you be among that percentage and miss a pay cheque, you would not be able to eat. For some of the scammers making the calls that plague the Western world, the choice may well be between defrauding us and not being able to feed their families. It's for that reason we should leave our judgement for the scam kingpins who are really coining it behind all of this misery, likely living in gated mansions outside India's urban centres, or even abroad. Next time you receive a scam call from a South Asian voice, think about the choices the

< 36 >

person on the other end of the line might be facing and perhaps blame their boss or the owner of the business they're working for before you give them an earful.

Another angle worthy of our consideration in terms of the self-justification being applied by those making the calls is the status of Kolkata as one of India's largest scam call hubs in terms of call volume. The previous home of the East India Company, for many decades it was used by Britain to extract resources from our new colony and enrich our country. There is a certain irony that this city is now the origin of so many scams that try to transfer the wealth back.

The top-voted comment from an Indian member of the public on a recent *Times of India* report related to scam call centres, perhaps giving a sense of where much public opinion in India related to scammer culture lands. It suggested that scammers calling from their country should 'focus their attention on the UK, as it is the UK that looted trillions of dollars from India'.

If this opinion is anything to go by, and with a Hindu nationalist government in place under Narendra Modi, the likelihood of political sympathy for British victims of phone call scams, and associated action, seems unlikely to happen any time soon. Without more serious technological and legislative solutions being considered at our end, we may be stuck with the problem of scam calls originating in this part of the world for a good many years yet.

⊕ WEST AFRICA – FROM NIGERIAN PRINCE TO GHANAIAN HUSBAND

West Africa, particularly Nigeria, may well be the first region that comes into people's minds when we think of email scams, thanks to one of the oldest scams of the internet age – the 'Nigerian Prince' scam. It's a very basic form of advanced fee fraud, beginning in the earliest days of email

< 37 >

as scammers realized the opportunity to send messages internationally and entirely free of charge.

Broadly speaking (and more on this later in Chapter 4: Email Scams), it goes like this – you receive an email claiming to be from the executor of a rich Nigerian prince who has died and bequeathed some money to you. It sounds sensational because it's millions of dollars. All you need to do to secure the funds is to help the executor or lawyer with a small fee to release the money.

It's a unique concept, featuring a succession of known scam techniques, including a lure (your portion of the millions of dollars) and an advanced fee (the small price you must pay to secure it), never mind the fact that this comes totally out of the blue and it's highly likely you won't have any idea why a dead Nigerian royal might have you in their will. You may rightly be asking yourself how on earth this came to be the speciality of early-internet Nigerian emailers? Why Nigeria? It's a good question and essentially just comes down to scammers in Nigeria being first to it.

The scam itself has a history of hundreds of years. Before it was known as a Nigerian Prince scam, it was called the Spanish Prisoner scam, the earliest versions of which can be traced back to letters sent during the French Revolution. The themes are broadly similar: a Spanish nobleman requests your assistance in securing their release from prison. Should you be able to help, they will shower you with riches and ensure that you are never wanting for money again. They require a bail payment/lawyer's fees or similar to be able to get out. Should you pay up, you receive another letter detailing issues with the release, more money is needed to secure it, and this goes on and on for as long as you are willing to keep paying.

No one can be entirely certain how this concept made its way into the hands of Nigerian scammers, but it is not unlikely that it began as a fraud conducted by traditional mail before pivoting with the emergence of an internet café culture in the country in the late 1990s. As the internet first arrived in Nigeria around that time, a drop in oil prices had caused

< 38 >

extremely difficult economic conditions in the country. At an internet café, getting online was relatively cheap.

Some of those who were out of work, or who never found any work after leaving school or graduating, instead entered a different kind of school – one where your friends and older members of your immediate family taught you how to scam people online. These early adopters probably worked out that they could repurpose the Spanish prisoner into something that made sense to them, and once they realized it worked (because at that point no one had heard of a Nigerian Prince scam), it effectively went viral.

So large-scale and so successful were the early days of the Nigerian Prince scam in the late '90s and early '00s that the people who did it got their own nickname: 419 scammers. The 419 relates back to the section of the Nigerian penal code which concerns fraud. For many religious Nigerians, the name also conveniently fit into the Bible's Book of Psalms, 4:19: 'Yea, mine own familiar friend, in whom I trusted, which did eat of my bread, hath lifted his heel against me.'

Seeing the success of the early 419 scammers, the culture of scamming in Nigeria started to appeal to a wider group. From a criminal underworld it expanded to include frustrated, young, educated men who found that the job market in a country whose economy had been ruined by corruption and years of military dictatorship wasn't rewarding them. Now, over two decades into the life of 419 scammer culture, the Nigerian Prince has evolved into all manner of different scams across the country and has further expanded into nearby Ghana. The Nigerian and Ghanaian scammers of today don't hesitate to flaunt their successes on social media, posting pictures of their houses, cars and piles of cash obtained by defrauding victims. Just like in the West, the culture of both countries glamorizes wealth, and this lifestyle obviously appeals to young people suffering the same economic issues as their older relatives in the '90s and '00s, so recruitment is made easy for the scam networks – and so the cycle continues.

< 39 >

That cycle is perpetuated in Ghana particularly by the presence of what is known in the Ghanaian scam community as 'HK', short for Hustle Kingdom. HK is, in essence, a scam school. According to those in the know, there are several established across the country. They are controlled by senior scammers, who pass on their skills to a younger generation of students. You have to pay to attend, and it's highly likely that some of the students do so by agreeing to hand over a large percentage of their future earnings from the scams they are taught. Once the students 'graduate', they are drawn into the employment of a larger scam syndicate, which pools money and provides employee benefits like accommodation and food.

The work of the West African scammer is also broadly accepted by many in their communities – to some, it is seen as a positive to defraud Westerners, essentially payback for the appalling damage done to this part of the world by slavery. There is a clear parallel between this and the feelings in India mentioned above. There are plenty of ordinary Ghanaians and Nigerians for whom taking money from a white person by deception is not a morally questionable act but an honourable one atoning for the ills of the past, even a civic duty to help the less fortunate. This leads to many skilled scammers becoming respected members of their communities, giving portions of their earnings back to the hungry and poor, supporting those around them through scams.

So baked-in is the industry of scamming in Nigeria and Ghana that it has now become intertwined with even more historical elements of the culture of these countries, including spiritualism and juju. In some areas of both countries, scammers perform juju rituals to bless themselves with luck before their day's work begins, invoking spells, holding charms or amulets and chanting, as they believe it will help them control their victims, make money flow their way or protect them from law enforcement. This binding of scam culture and the ancient culture of the land only adds to the potent mystique and intrigue that surrounds scammers in both Ghana and Nigeria.

< 40 >

The scams, which now most commonly come from West Africa, aren't Nigerian Prince emails, though – they are romance scams, or catfishing scams. Why romance? Quite simply, the widespread and multi-generational use of social media in the global north has made it very easy to find victims. Equally, romance scams can (mostly) be played out via text – and while English language proficiency in Nigeria and Ghana is good, particularly if a person is educated to a reasonable level, their accent could be a giveaway if they are posing as a woman from Canada or a man from the UK.

A romance scam network in Ghana (where they are known as Sakawa Boys, or 'Putting Inside' Boys in English, translated from the Hausa language spoken in part of Ghana) or Nigeria (where the groups running romance scams are known as Yahoo Boys, due to their common use of Yahoo.com email addresses) recruits young, frustrated men, mostly from poorer, rural communities. New starters are set up with a social media profile, either one they have created themselves or one that has been hacked using stolen username and password combinations bought on the dark web. A hacked profile is better because it will have pre-existing friends, photos and a posting history likely going back years, making it almost impossible for anyone interacting with it to know that the person behind the profile isn't who they seem.

With their profile ready to go, they begin joining singles groups on social media sites, dating platforms and forums, the likes of which can be found in their millions all over the online world. Next, they start talking to people. To all intents and purposes, they seem like they might be a great candidate to start a relationship with; inevitably, they use profiles of good-looking people of all ages but adjust them to pique the maximum amount of interest they can from potential victims. To do so, they might begin by giving their fake selves fascinating and usually dangerous jobs, like working as a diver repairing oil rigs or in the military. These jobs will almost always involve spending prolonged periods abroad or in areas

< 41 >

where it is difficult to communicate by conventional methods like the phone. This is the perfect cover to explain why it is they can't talk on the phone or take a video call with their new friend.

Each individual scammer will be working from a script, either a literal document sent by their overseers and containing all the information they need to make a scam work, or if they are working alone they will simply use the passed-on knowledge from whoever it was who taught them how to scam. It begins with what's known as 'love-bombing', essentially making contact with a possible victim and in the early days of the relationship showering them with contact, compliments and expressions of excitement at what this new friendship might bring.

From the love-bombing stage they will then begin what's known as 'seeding' – essentially planting ideas early on in the getting-to-know-you period, which will then be used to call back on later as justification for their requests for money. For example, should they have a very dangerous job welding underwater on oil rigs, when they suffer an injury at work and due to some misfortune can't pay their medical bill, it won't seem entirely unusual that they ask for your assistance in helping with the money.

These relationships and the trust-gaining period may go on weeks before requests for money are involved. When they do begin, they will relate back to something the scammer flagged earlier in their dialogue with the victim. The requests will always be one of two things and sometimes a combination of them:

1. Time critical, in that the money must be sent in the very near future.

2. Emotionally charged, for example related to the child of the scammer's fake persona or their own physical health.

< 42 >

What this means is that not only do the monetary requests seem reasonable, as they are related to seeded subject matter from early in the victim's relationship with them, they also play on the victim's humanity, making them feel that they are being a good person by helping out. The scammer will always promise that they will return the money as soon as they can.

The time-critical nature of these requests will also make the victim operate outside of what we would call their 'rational mind'. This is how you would use your brain when in a normal mood or state, considering a big decision like sending money somewhere. If you are ready to be irrational due to time pressure, are having feelings of guilt about being a good person to your new-found friend and are emotionally involved with them on top of all that, it makes for a very persuasive mix indeed.

Finally, to secure you as theirs and theirs alone, the romance scammer will attempt to isolate you from any sources of support you might have in your life, like friends or family. If you mention the idea of telling them about your new relationship, the romance scammer will attempt to put you off this idea by suggesting it shows you are doubtful and that you do not trust them as they trust you, again employing guilt as a weapon against you. This combination of psychological tactics are fundamentally why romance scams are so successful in extorting large amounts of money from their victims.

Worse still, the longer you have been in a romance scam, the harder it will be to get out. Having invested emotionally over a long period, the last thing you will want to do is admit to yourself that you have indeed been duped and abused by this person you have feelings for. These scams work so well because we hate to admit to ourselves that we were wrong, especially when it comes to love.

To better understand what the scam business looks like in today's West Africa and the lives of the people behind the social media profiles, I wanted to speak to those using them, to obtain testimony from currently

< 43 >

working romance scammers and 419 scammers. Finding them would not be difficult – in fact, they came to me, approaching me out of the blue on social media, hiding behind profiles of attractive women, hoping I'd be their next victim.

It's quite clear that they don't check profiles (otherwise I wouldn't get these messages, given that my bio states I'm a scam expert), but it worked out well. Over time, I explained my role and exchanged messages with the scammers, and eventually I gained their trust. The written testimonies which follow all come from genuine scammers who just happened to message me out of the blue to try a scam, across various social media platforms.

In the interests of full disclosure, they were paid for their contributions – about £120 each. When you are working with scammers, it's incredibly difficult to persuade them that putting their head above the parapet on any level is a good idea, never mind doing so to provide testimony for a book about scams! Despite doing what they do remotely, this group at least are clearly still a bit worried about being caught.

While it would have been preferable, and their words perhaps carried more weight had they been willing to do it for free, I agreed to pay all of them for their time. A very interesting thing happened once I had paid the first of them – 'Cody' – to write for me. Suddenly, I had so many approaches on social media from romance scammers and 419 scammers, seemingly just happening to find me and start their scam, I was spoilt for choice. Even more interestingly, they would give up the ghost on their scam almost immediately, claiming they had read my profile and wanted to ask me some questions. Sure enough, the conversation soon turned to the prospect of them being willing to tell me a bit about what they do professionally and about their lives. It seemed that word had got around the scam community in West Africa that there was a man paying for their stories, and that the money was pretty good.

< 44 >

To further gain their trust, I created a process by which they could send me their testimony without worrying too much about the authorities ever seeing it. They would create an entirely clean, brand-new email address that had never been used, in a fake name. They would write their testimonies in an internet café or using a computer with a virtual private network and send them to my encrypted email using that computer. My email is encrypted to protect my sources and those who send me their stories; essentially, this means the data is safe from prying eyes, including the authorities, unless I give someone the password.

Below are the testimonies sent to me by those currently working as scammers in West Africa who agreed to my terms. Whether they are genuine accounts of their lives, how they work and their true feelings only they will know, but they do certainly fit with what we know about the industry. I choose to believe them because these four at least I spent a good amount of time talking to before they agreed to do this, and given the protections in place I don't particularly see what reason they would have to lie. I have only edited them where I felt it was necessary to make the meaning clear, and I checked my edits with all of them before adding them to the book. These are their words …

'CODY', NIGERIAN LIVING IN GHANA, THIRTIES

I didn't really face much stress or challenges growing up because I have a good dad helping me with what I needed in school, right from my elementary school until college. He believed school was the greatest accomplishment I could have in life. He always gave a little out of his pocket for my allowance because we are a family of six. I didn't have much on my own, but Dad was supportive until my graduation. I graduated as a BSC holder in agricultural economics.

I had a dream of getting out of school and becoming someone reputable because everything about my dad and my career was about graduating from college. It left me with not much dreams until I became a college graduate. I've never worked anywhere after I finished school because I left my state for another state right after school to get a good job, but all I was offered as a graduate in the capital Lagos was a security job or a cleaning job in a hotel.

If you've ever been to Nigeria, you'll realize that in Lagos, where companies and opportunities are in, they have no job for graduates except a cleaner job. If you don't have a connection then you can't have a job. That leads me to scamming people to get money to pay bills.

First time scamming will never be easy. Months and years may pass by and you won't even have money to pay phone bills and you definitely will be discouraged and disappointed that it doesn't pay. With commitment and consistency without relent that's when maybe you can make some money. Sometimes even when money comes you don't see it because the person who you wanted to give you the payment may tell you he couldn't change it to your currency so you lost.

I got into scam because of how corrupt my country became. Nigeria, my country, is a country where there's no law and order. You do whatever you want and go free if you have money and connections. No good governance and so much hunger in the country, siblings and parents call from the village for assistance financially and you in the big city have nothing to offer. It looks as though you've been trained all through school to become useless.

Since you want to pay bills and have a little good life for yourself, you have no choice than to join whatever is trending that's making you get money to send to your parents and siblings suffering at home. Some even go to an extent of doing rituals and sacrifices to make the money start flowing. But it was friends who introduced me to scamming originally.

< 46 >

I use a military format for scamming. You look for a client that you go into relationship with online, introduce yourself as a military personnel and you went for peace keeping somewhere in Somalia or in a place where there's war. You don't make call because you're always at the war front, so the little time I have I can profess my love to my so-called spouse and use the avenue to get enough money from them because we don't call, we only message because of the nature of my work. We keep getting money from the spouse and never come back home or see them until they get tired and stop sending money.

I really feel bad sometimes about who I take money from. But I don't feel bad when I see the money because it pays bills I couldn't afford being a cleaner or a security. It's paying the bills and so I can't feel bad when I'm paying bills or have money. But deep down I feel bad that what I'm doing is wrong. Let me tell you that though, most of my friends and so many others see it like it's a punishment on the white folks because it's a payback for what they did to our forefathers, enslaving them for a long time and using them like rags until they got their independence.

I feel good when I'm scamming, without even seeing someone or negotiating a business physically, nor calling, but just by writing. It makes me know that I didn't go to school for nothing. It tells me that I would be a good and successful entrepreneur and a good businessman if I was given the opportunity. Regardless of what the client loses, I still feel fulfilled.

Looking at me physically, you'll realize I'm very funny and fun to be with. I'm an upcoming comedian and I'm waiting for a good opportunity to get to perform someday in a hall full of crowd and make my dreams come true. But before you get to that in my country, you got to have enough money to pay the ones at the top. Talents if not known in this country by people that matter are useless. I have a page I'm running as a comedian but I'm yet to hit the jackpot.

< 47 >

'BAYO', NIGERIAN LIVING IN IBADAN, TWENTIES

My name is Bayo, I am from the western part of Nigeria in Oyo State. My life wasn't easy growing up as my father was married to three wives. My mom was the third wife and I am the last born of my siblings, which are three. I'm living in the capital of Oyo State, which is Ibadan. I'm in my late twenties. My mom had to struggle with my siblings because my dad neglected his duties of taking care of us. Mom is dead, so I struggled for my tertiary institution through a polytechnic with an OND [Ordinary National Diploma] in laboratory science. I came from a poor background.

I have a dream of becoming a pharmacist when I was growing up. Until today I still want to be a pharmacist but haven't gone back to school ever since I started with the scamming. I intend going back to school to have my HND [Higher National Diploma] certificate as a lab scientist though. About my work, there's not much work to do in Nigeria than jobs meant for unskilled people except you have someone who knows someone to give you a good job. I don't have any good job but I've worked in a bakery once, and I worked as a fuel attendant in a gas station. I worked at some restaurants and bars, but I don't work any more.

I got into scams because of the challenges in the country. Our president is not a man we can count on. Promises are being failed by him. In as much as you are learned and skilful in whatsoever you do in the country, we still have nothing because we aren't given opportunities to do anything. We have a very bad governance in my country and so me trying to make ends meet gets me into scamming. I don't feel cool with that but it pays some bills if not all.

My scamming process and format is about government grants. It comes directly as a message through social medias to anyone, telling him or her about federal government grants that comes to citizens and that they can apply for the grant and get the money sent to them to their doorstep. Not many are interested, but some get so interested because

< 48 >

the money for the grant can range from $50,000 to $80,000 and so because of their greed, they then send money through me as an agent to apply for the government grant. They keep sending this money for delivery of the cash and so many processes comes as they pay until they can pay no more for the grant delivery.

In my innermost mind, I know it's wrong and I hate doing scams, but looking at my mates in high school having a house of their own, eating a good food, driving their own cars and wearing what they even couldn't afford gets me influenced into scamming. Bills from all angles gets me into scamming. With all of this going on, I just feel that scamming would be the only way to get money, so I don't feel bad at all when I scam.

What I earn depends on who I meet. You do business and you'll understand better that it's not all time you have your business going smoothly. I can earn $10,000 this month and not get any money until maybe the next six months to a year, so what I earn depends on who I meet at the course of the hustle. It's not specific. So the highest money I've earned for the past one year was $20,000.

I feel cool when I succeed bro. Takes months to get some kinda money so when you have it at last, why would you not be happy? You do business and then at last the business was concluded and money comes in, you just have to sit back and enjoy what you suffered for. It's not easy manipulating or convincing people to pay you money bro. I feel cool! My condition financially is not so stable per se, but I acquired what I know I can use to take care of myself for some time, and then I don't rest but keep grinding so I get more. I can say I have the money to be able to pay bills I couldn't pay when I was broke.

I watched my mom die because of some kind of sickness that drugs could stop or maybe extend her lifespan. They were expensive then for someone from a poor home like me to purchase for her since my dad couldn't cater for us cus of his polygamous family. I still want to go back to school. I really wish I could be a pharmacist, be able to innovate ideas

< 49 >

on drugs that can break into markets and help people, especially women. All of these will involve money and no one is willing to support you so I just hustle to get enough for all my dreams.

'JOHN', GHANAIAN LIVING IN ACCRA, TWENTIES

When I was five years old I started my schooling and I enjoy going until secondary school. At eighteen I step down after I finished my secondary school because my parents are poor and can't afford to help me pay for university.

My hobbies as a child were playing football and watching football games. I supported Manchester United because I admired Cristiano Ronaldo. My family is not rich but at least we can afford daily meals. I have two siblings which are girls, I am the only son of my father so there is pressure on me to make money.

After finishing school I have been finding way to get money at least so I can be able to help my parents and so I can go back to college or university. I found work with a manufacturing company here in my state and I have been paid around $25 monthly, which is not enough for me to help my family and pay my bills.

After five months working like this, my friends refer me to their scamming group and I was taught how to operate through the Facebook app and scam for money. It is not out of willingness that I am scamming for money but for some of us, our family background and country economy gives us no choice. Now I have learned the Facebook scamming called dating, I operate alone in my room trying to collect money from white men. I earn more than $300 every month with just my phone. My biggest scam is $500 in a single day.

I study social science in my secondary school and I dream of becoming a computer engineer because I am very good when it comes to computer

< 50 >

science, that is my goal for life. My family never knew that I scammed for money because I always hide it from them. I live in a single room away from my community. I want to quit scamming if I can get government support or personal support, but I can't live without it at the moment. When you are scamming you always have the fear of being caught and it could end up your life in prison.

It is a risk to earn money to live, that's why I will risk my life to scam white men.

'FREDDIE', UGANDAN LIVING IN SWITZERLAND, THIRTIES

I grew up as a child with determination of being an independent entrepreneur. I was born in Uganda and raised there. Mummy is a civil servant, she taught at high school level. Growing up wasn't funny – I passed through a lot of difficult things, but thankfully, I'm still alive.

My dad who abused alcohol, he would kick our pets without sympathy and threaten to kill my mum. He was sent to prison and is dead now. My dream was to be able to provide whatever I want for myself and my family, my friends or even helping those who need it.

I love listening to music. My favourite songs are Dolly Parton 'Coat of Many Colors', Luther Vandross 'Dance with My Father', Ed Sheeran 'Visiting Hours' and Elton John 'Sacrifice'. I like writing stories, I'm a skilful writer, and I also enjoy painting.

I've been scammed. It was a fake investment platform on the internet. I believed they would return me huge interest plus the capital I put in. In three hours from when I started I got blocked, immediately after the transfer was made through Bitcoin. I thought to commit suicide afterwards but could not do it.

The most successful scam I have done was one thousand pounds. I

< 51 >

was very happy when the money was successfully taken, but in the other way I feel very uncomfortable considering who was actually scammed. I feel I have no other choice than doing this work because I have to pay and also maintain myself and the family as a first child. I can still feel bad for doing this work, like when I scammed an old woman from Manchester in 2019 because she's a poor widow and can barely take care of her bills then and she finally passed away.

There are eight scammers in the group I work with. Working as a team has given us an opportunity to share new ideas with each other, and to make people believe whatever we say seems to be right and we make huge amount of money in that way on a daily basis. I want to be responsibly rich so I can meet my goals and also be able to contribute towards the community or a society as a whole. Looking at the world or the community today, the reality of what exactly happened is that the rich want to be richer, they are not thinking about the less privileged or the masses as a whole. It touches me deeply.

Probably more people are interested in becoming scammers but surely I know it is going to stop once the right thing is done by our leaders. Creating job opportunities for the people, especially the youth, empowering them with good education and technical experiences, making them experts on what they want to do in life will totally change their lives and mindset so they don't want to become scammers any more.

Few people are aware of what I do but I have no choice, because I'm able to raise some money to feed the younger ones in my family and try to help a few other people as a means of support.

Back in 2015, I worked as a software engineer. My mum got sick and no one was there to look after her, and my employer failed to grant me permission to go and help her. Then I disobeyed the boss, because life is priceless, I went to my mum. They sacked me and left me with nothing, which is why I started scamming. But my background as a software engineer really built me up and upgraded my ability to

< 52 >

scam people around the globe now. My main field of scam is selling of fake properties, cars, houses and lots of household equipment which I sell online. The person I'm scamming pays me a deposit but wouldn't see anything or neither hear back from my end once I have their money.

　　　　　■　　■　　■

Heartless criminals? Victims of circumstance? How do you feel having read the testimonies of these four scammers? Whether or not you believe them is entirely up to you, but hopefully they help to illuminate the motivations of those working in the scam industry.

Perhaps if the opportunities offered in the countries they live in were better, they would not have felt that they had little choice but to turn to this kind of work. The combination of that and the reality of the modern internet-connected world, where contact with the comparatively better-off people of the West is easy, and the likelihood of actually being caught and sent to prison so small, has made the lures of the 419 scam and the romance scam too great for many young men (and some women) in parts of Africa to resist.

A registered nurse in Ghana can make about $200 a month, after years of university and training get them to the place where they're ready to do this incredibly taxing and stressful job. If you're a young person without much education and can save enough to buy yourself a smartphone, you can make more than that in a month from your bedroom, with nothing more than a social media app and a script. It gets the bills paid and means you can send some money to your family; you can even have a decent standard of living compared to your peers who don't scam people.

It's always easy to sit in judgement, but if we're honest with ourselves, had you or I been born in Ghana or Nigeria, it's entirely plausible that we might be romance scammers or 419 scammers too.

< 53 >

⊕ SOUTH-EAST ASIA –
THE FUTURE OF FRAUD

What's in my view without doubt the single most profitable and fastest growing scam on the planet is also the one with the most disgusting name: the pig butchering scam. The somewhat disturbing title of this particular ruse relates to its origins in China, where the phrase 'Sha Zhu Pan' was given to describe it (literally translated as 'Pig Killing Plate'). Why pigs? Because in China, and elsewhere, you fatten up the pig before you kill it. That perfectly encapsulates what they do in this scam.

Originating in China around 2016 and almost certainly backed by Chinese organized crime, it is also a distinctly modern scam in a few ways: it has big money behind it; it can be run almost entirely by text messages alone; and the worst/best part depending on which side you come from, the entire planet is your potential victim.

When you know that this scam's potential customer is the entire world, the idea of it making as much as £10 billion globally in a year doesn't seem so shocking. In fact, it's almost certainly an underestimation. So, how does what is potentially the world's most successful single scam work? It's a tweaked-for-improvement mixture of a romance scam and an investment scam that plays a long game. As a possible victim, you might have no sense at all that you're being 'fattened up' until you've been speaking to the scammer for weeks, even months.

It all begins (as so many of these scams do) with an out-of-the-blue message. This may be a wrong number, seemingly innocent, asking to connect after you met at a party. When you explain that you believe they have the wrong number, you will get a somewhat awkward request to be friends in spite of the error. I've had them myself; they might use the profile picture of a good-looking young woman or man to tempt you into saying yes.

Should you decide to entertain them, you'll quickly find yourself in the early stages of classic romance scam tactics: love-bombing through

< 54 >

regular and intense contact, endless compliments and flirtation. You might really feel like you're starting to connect with this person. They will start to share more pictures of themselves too, perhaps even videos of them coquettishly saying hello or blowing kisses. This can continue for weeks on end. The scripts used by pig butchering groups are not unknown to run to sixty or even 100 pages of A4. This ensures that the character you are interacting with – because that is ultimately what they are, a fantasy created to push all the right buttons of any potential partner – has incredible depth. There will be answers ready for almost any question you have for them, from the mundane to the deeply personal.

At some point you will inevitably discuss work. Here, the seeding of their future attempt to scam you will begin: they might casually drop in that they do a bit of investing on the side and that's how they make most of their money, despite having a full-time job. There won't be any further discussion of it, though, just a casual mention.

Weeks down the line they might revisit the topic again, dropping into your conversations their excitement at how much money they made using the trading platform they prefer that week, even sending a screen grab of their vast weekly take on a few trades. At this point, they will ask if you've ever considered doing the same. If you have some savings that aren't making extra money for you, why not put them to work?

This is where the real work begins for the scammer. If you start to have questions at this point in proceedings, the pig butchering group will have every reassurance imaginable available for you. It might involve, for example, a quick video call with your new love interest. This is possible because the most successful pig butchering scammers have evolved beyond using stolen photos and videos taken from online influencers or models. Why would you do that when you've got the money to bombproof your scam by employing a model of your own full time?

That's right: at the higher end of the pig butchering scam scale, they hire in models and employ them on a full-time wage. What this means is, at your

< 55 >

deepest moments of insecurity and mistrust of this new love interest's ideas about investing in cryptocurrency, or foreign exchange trading, or whatever it might be, they will be happy to have an actual video call with you.

This new weapon in the arsenal of the scammer makes it virtually impossible to be sure that you're dealing with a fake. All your text conversations will be conducted with someone paid far less than the model, and the model will be having video calls with different 'customers' like you all day. The group will probably employ tens or even hundreds of people to run the script by text, all pretending to be the same model. The model will just have to make videos and photos and take video calls from those victims who are wobbling or not buying into the scam.

With you reassured by your video call and likely entirely absorbed in the scam, your new friend – who you are completely convinced is a real person, because they are, just not the person you think – will offer to help you with investing in the way that they do. At this point, they will walk you through the entire process of setting up an account and investing on the platform they have shown you they use (there will be more detail on how this works later in the book).

More often than not, these platforms are entirely developed and created by scammers. They are essentially a smoke-and-mirrors website designed to reflect that your investment (however much it might be) is doing incredibly well. Week on week, they may even let you take a small amount of money out of the pot to genuinely realize some profit: the goal is to encourage you to invest more.

The most serious groups have gone so far as to make promotional videos for their investment platform, with beautifully animated charts and graphics explaining in layman's terms exactly how it all supposedly works. They might even have a referral system by which you can invite your friends to join the platform, offering you financial bonuses for each person who joins and in doing so turning their romance scam–investment scam mix into a pyramid scheme as well.

< 56 >

The genius of this, unfortunately, is that it all seems to function and be set up exactly like any genuine online investment website. Your chances of realizing it's a scam if you aren't already in that world are vanishingly small. Once they have got you hooked with your imaginary massive returns, your friend will keep encouraging you to put more and more money in. After all, the more they take, the more they get paid themselves, as pig butchering scammers, like many others in this world, are paid commission.

One day, perhaps months after all this started, when the scammer thinks they have taken you for all you've got, you'll go to log in to your investment website and check on your funds. Either it won't exist at all, or your login won't work. Panicked, you'll likely head over to your messaging app, or whatever dating website you met your new friend on. Their profile will also be gone, all your thousands of messages deleted – it's like they never existed at all.

The chances of getting any of your money back from this scam are almost zero. It is highly likely that your initial payments will have been paid into a cryptocurrency platform, where you were encouraged to set up an account in your name before being sent on to what you believed was your investment website. This means that from your bank's perspective you were sending money (initially at least) to yourself, which is a defence for them against returning money to you. From there the money was converted into cryptocurrency and sent on to another cryptocurrency wallet, with you believing it was headed into your investment account. Likewise, the cryptocurrency platform providing the wallet is unlikely to take responsibility for where you chose to send your money.

Sadly, the scammers are making money hand over fist using this method. If you want documented indicators of just how successful this scam has become beyond the figures, *Scam Interceptors'* own Jim Browning has a fantastic video on the subject on his YouTube channel, Tech Support Scams. It demonstrated how one group, based out of Dubai but again run by a Chinese gang, employed hundreds of scammers from countries like Syria, all of them living and working in four high-rise blocks about half an hour outside the city.

This is devious on two levels. Firstly, half an hour outside of Dubai you find yourself in the middle of a desert, so should the authorities decide they would like to raid you, it is quite literally possible to see them coming a mile away. Secondly, your 'employees', who you have bussed in from the city, can't leave without your help – they are effective prisoners in their place of work.

Sadly for those roped into this line of work, this is a common theme. So common in fact that in the global epicentre of this type of crime, South-East Asia, the United Nations believe that almost a quarter of a million people may currently be 'working' as indentured labour, trafficked into scam compounds on false pretences to run a variety of scams including pig butchering.

It makes one scam compound in Dubai with hundreds of employees sound like small fry. In the Philippines, a single raid resulted in 2,700 indentured 'workers' being freed, and if you ask China, their authorities believe as many as 400,000 Chinese nationals might be working for cyber fraud organizations in South-East Asia.

The brutal criminal industry behind the pig butchering scams is as cruel to those running them as it is to its victims. Conditions for the unfortunate people caught in scam compounds across South-East Asia range from bad to inhumane, to life-threatening. The vast majority are either ethnically Chinese, from rural communities with low education, or from surrounding countries where employment opportunities are limited, like Malaysia, Vietnam and Cambodia. Tempted by exotic-sounding job adverts for telesales positions in neighbouring nations posted on job websites, with good pay and benefits, they sign up willingly.

On arrival at their new place of work, all is not as it was promised to be, with the expected gleaming office block in reality a prison compound

< 58 >

of high-rise flats surrounded by high walls and razor wire, entrances and exits manned by armed guards. The soon-to-be scammers find themselves scammed from the start. In Myanmar, entire towns like Shwe Kokko have become dedicated pig butchering facilities. In Cambodia, particularly in the beach resort of Sihanoukville, numerous former casino resorts have been converted to house scammers.

Before the pandemic, Sihanoukville was the centre of gambling in Cambodia, a sort of seat-of-the-pants version of Macau, where everything was slightly more affordable. The combination of the pandemic's devastating effects on tourism and Cambodia's somewhat despotic government deciding it didn't like gambling any more suddenly made the casinos of Sihanoukville redundant. Their owners, interesting types from China and Taiwan with nicknames like 'Big Fatty', needed to find a way to make their enormous investments pay again.

As it happens, filling a hotel with computers and desks and turning hotel rooms into permanent accommodation for a slave army of scammers proved a highly cost-effective way of doing so. Stick some bunk beds into the rooms, clear furniture out of the others and replace it with classic office cubicles and screens. Set up a canteen in the old restaurant to keep your workers fed.

If you're practiced in the ways of the organized criminal world, keeping your employees on site through a regime of threats, actual physical violence and torture is not so hard either. Should you be more into coercive methods of control, just take away their phones and passports on arrival and keep them there until their visas run out. At that point the threat of immigration difficulties should be enough of a deterrent to ensure their obedience.

You've always got the carrot rather than the stick as well, so you can dangle the possibility of getting their travel documents and devices back, plus a cash bonus if they hit their targets during a week's worth of sixteen-hour shifts. Worst comes to worst, if your employee really isn't cut out for

< 59 >

this kind of work, you can always contact their family and ransom them for tens of thousands of pounds.

That's the life of the vast majority of pig butchering scammers, paid a pittance to try to sign up victims across the world for their boss's enormous benefit, largely in fear of their lives or at least under threat of appalling harm from their employer. There are countless documented examples of this across South-East Asia, as well as more anecdotal reports of scammers being shot when trying to escape and committing suicide. The 'Chinatown' scam compound in Sihanoukville is known locally as a place where it's unusual if an ambulance doesn't turn up at least a couple of times every week.

The gigantic wave of human misery on both sides of a pig butchering scam is almost incalculable and sadly constantly expanding in size. The technological advancements that have made it possible have also allowed for this scam to develop into a truly global phenomenon which is not showing any sign of relenting, despite attention from international law enforcement. The gangs behind this scam choose carefully where they operate and it's not in countries that have an open and honest relationship with either the Western world's law enforcement authorities, or anywhere else's for that matter. Myanmar is under a military junta, Cambodia is a despotic regime. Both countries will be full of officials and diplomats who do not make it difficult for groups as wealthy as the pig butchering scammers to pay them off handsomely to look the other way. Examples like the compound in Dubai are few and far between. Even then, provided the scammers don't go after victims from the country they're based in, the ruling powers are highly unlikely to act without diplomatic pressure from elsewhere.

As if all that wasn't bad enough, guess where some of these truly appalling operations are laundering all their money? That's right – the UK. Using limited companies set up in Britain on Companies House to take payment and run their funds through, adding a veil of legitimacy to their vile crime.

< 60 >

Part of the reason why these pig butchering scams are so successful is that the entire world is your potential customer. The development of live translation software, though well intentioned, has proved to be incredibly useful in this type of scam. Where previously the pig butchering scam groups would have needed to employ people with a good grasp of English, now they can hire almost anyone from anywhere, with almost any level of education. It gives them the ability to employ the cheapest, most vulnerable people imaginable. Pretty much everyone on the planet can read messages and cut and paste answers from a script.

What the software further allows is for the user to build in their instant messaging account, type in messages in their own language and for them to appear on the receiver's screen in a language of their choosing. For example, the pig butchering scammer could employ a Cambodian, who is typing in their own language of Khmer, speaking to a Hungarian, who is receiving the messages on their screen almost as if they are coming from a Hungarian native. I have watched that exact interaction happen. This expands the potential victim pool of the pig butchering operations to be virtually every single person on Planet Earth. There is no human being they would not be able to try to run their scam on, provided they have money and an internet connection, and that frightening prospect is surely the future of fraud.

⊕ THE UK/US – HI MUM, GOODBYE MONEY

No tour of the global business of scams and fraud would be complete without a stop in the Western world. While we might like to comfort ourselves by blaming other countries for the explosion of this type of crime, similar offences are happening within our own borders as well.

Much of what the scammers in the West do is essentially copycat operations on what they have seen successfully run by others elsewhere in

< 61 >

the world, be that a British take on a bank impersonation scam started by a well-mannered cold call from a reassuringly homely accent, organized crime groups pretending to be the financial authorities seeking unpaid tax or buying products using stolen debit card details obtained from a card skimmer installed in a cashpoint (ATM). The scale and depth of Western fraud culture is such that it has developed its own language to describe certain acts, products and people. A victim is a *vic*, as in 'he looks like a vic'; someone's personal information, card details and PIN number are *fullz*, as in full details.

In 2019, a book was released online, initially to buy but eventually for free, titled *The Fraud Bible*. This 124-page document spells out exactly how you would start up and run a vast array of scams and frauds, from exploits on websites allowing you to steal products like video games free of charge to a guide on 'eWhoring', which involves posing as attractive women online and selling imaginary used underwear to interested men.

So enamoured with *The Fraud Bible* were those using it, US rapper Lil Thony wrote a whole song about it, the inventively named 'Fraud Bible'. The fraud scene in the UK and US has become just as glamorized among the disenfranchised young as it is in West Africa – arguably more so – and the concept of scamming for money is now intertwined with music culture favoured by those who run scams. Drill, a subgenre of gangster rap which grew out of Chicago in the 2010s and is now hugely popular in the UK, is synonymous with fraud. There's another subgenre in the US, also inventively named: Scam Rap.

There are even 'scamfluencers', individuals whose online personas were so popular despite being synonymous with scams that they have managed to co-opt that fame into a music career or a line of clothing, or some other product they can sell. Others have done it the other way around, initially gaining online fame for something entirely unrelated to scams, building a large online following of interested and dedicated people, which they quickly realize they can make money from.

< 62 >

One of the easiest ways is to run a scam. Popular TikTok lads who pivot from making videos of their efforts chatting up women to selling a course in foreign exchange trading, despite having no expertise in the matter whatsoever. Instagram glamour girls who suddenly become experts in cryptocurrency investment. You might as well ask a hamster for its thoughts on treating your bad back as pay these people for their advice on how to make money.

There is a spectrum of this type of character in the UK fraud scene. Tankz is the perfect example of the more criminal end. An anonymous young British man who describes himself as an 'Alleged Fraudstar/Artist and Influencer', he's turned apparently scamming people into a rap career and a relatively popular podcast. Tankz has a song called 'SFO (Serious Fraud Office)', about how the Serious Fraud Office supposedly tried to convict him, and he will sit happily in front of a camera on YouTube discussing how he believes scams to be a victimless crime, albeit while wearing a mask.

Public-facing companies and tradespeople running scams have comparatively been around for a very long time indeed. Making *Rogue Traders* for the best part of ten years taught me that there is an unending supply of seemingly honest people out there for whom making an honest living simply isn't enough.

We documented everything from plumbers who would do emergency work and then quote absurdly high prices to vulnerable older people, a company who claimed they could paint a product on your home's brickwork to bring your energy bills down (surprise, it was total nonsense), terrifying tree surgeons who would try distraction burglary while charging crazy money to butcher your garden and even pressure-selling photography studios preying on the hopes and dreams of those who wanted to become models. All these people are scammers too. Just because some had public-facing limited companies with well-heeled directors and nice offices in the UK doesn't make them any less criminal than those outside our shores.

< 63 >

Part Two

THE SCAM
COMPENDIUM

TELLS: MY SYSTEM FOR SNIFFING OUT SCAMS

In this part of the book you will find a list of every type of scam I have become aware of in my line of work. The scams are broken into loose categories based on where or how you might come across them and contain written explanations of how each scam works and why. The chapter openers themselves have quick pointers, four or five questions or actions that will save you should you find yourself encountering a scam of this type. When it comes to scams, speed of access to good advice helps, so mark out the pages with tabs of your own if you think they will help you find the right questions and actions quickly.

Within each chapter, you'll find comprehensive explanations of the types of scam that fall into each category. I have given them snappy names of my own, to try to help you remember them and so they hopefully spring into your mind when necessary. At the end of each scam, you will also find a short section I'm calling 'The Tells'.

A tell, in a game of poker, is an unconscious action that gives away your attempts to deceive another player. For example, your eyebrow twitches when you lie about your cards, or you look skyward after making a bet which is a bluff. In the world of scams, for me 'The Tells' are the signs you can read, the red flags and sometimes the psychological tricks the scammer uses to try to get you to pay out your money. I have categorized them and will list the tells which relate to each scam. Some will overlap, others have tells exclusive to them. Knowing what they are and being

< 67 >

able to recognize them will form a huge part of your suit of armour protecting you from scams.

Bear in mind that the scammers are coming up with new tricks, what they call 'updates', all the time. Many of these scams will have variations, alterations and entirely different narratives by the time you read this book, don't doubt that for a second. What they will have, however, is the same broad structure, the same tells. If you learn the tells and apply the advice to each possible scam you encounter, you'll be totally capable of seeing even an entirely new scam coming and able to deal with it appropriately.

Ultimately, if we all knew how to see these signs and had all of them in our heads ready to go, it would be much more difficult for the out-of-the-blue approach of most scammers to work. Their entire way of operating in the vast majority of cases relies upon catching you unawares – I hope this is going to make all of us much better prepared.

< 68 >

3

Phone Call Scams

Did this call come out of the blue?

Assume it's a scam.

Do you feel under pressure?

No legitimate caller would ever want you to feel pressurized. Take a breath.

Are you being asked to do anything you wouldn't normally do?

For example, are you being asked to make bank transfers or download software?

Is there anyone else you can ask if the call sounds right to them?

A second opinion always helps.

Tell the caller you will hang up and call back whoever they claim to represent on a number you will find yourself.

If they're a scammer, they'll do anything to keep you on the line. A legitimate organization will have no problem with this.

THE BANK IMPERSONATION SCAM

You receive a phone call, likely from a robotic voice telling you that transactions have been made on your account. It requests that if you did not make these transactions, you press 1 to speak to your card supplier's security department. The first red flag here is that responsibility for

< 69 >

fraudulent transactions is run by your bank – not by your card supplier.

The scammer, posing as your card supplier's security department, will begin by asking you various questions to 'verify' your identity. Their verification questions will involve asking for your bank's sort code and your account numbers. They may also ask you to retrieve a bank statement to give them your last closing balance. This is not information you should ever share over the phone.

The 'verification' is an information-gathering exercise for the scammers. It is scripted to make you feel as if they are on your side and there to help you stop someone spending your money without your consent. By handing over your sort code, the scammer will be able to use an online 'sort code checker' to find out which bank you opened your account with and the specific branch of that bank you opened it at. When the conversation started, they likely had no information about you at all beyond your phone number.

The scammer will then explain to you that they believe the imaginary transactions on your account are fraudulent. They will claim that they will then pass this information on to 'your bank's security department' and that you will receive a second phone call from them. Some may transfer you directly or give you a number to call instead.

In your conversation with this second scammer, posing as your actual bank's security department, they will explain that your specific local branch of your bank is currently the subject of an investigation by the bank's own security department for fraud. There is a rogue employee who has been supposedly spending your money. This story is intended to create trust between you and the scammer and remove the trust you have in your local bank. They will then request that you help the investigation. You must go to your local branch and request to withdraw funds as cash. This will be something in the region of £1,000–£10,000. Less than a thousand is too little for them to bother with, while over £10,000 is likely to see more serious questions asked by the bank.

The scammers will claim this helps their investigation by identifying

< 70 >

which employee at the local branch is engaging in fraud. They will likely request that you take this action the very same day, to avoid giving you too much time to think about it. They will also insist that what they have told you is to be kept entirely private and is not for sharing with anyone, to avoid you getting a second opinion.

If you agree to withdraw funds as requested, you'll be coached by the scammer in exactly what to say at the bank. They'll explain that you should state you're withdrawing the cash to pay a tradesperson for work on your house, or to buy a new car. Again, this is because they want you to avoid mentioning their phone call to anyone at all.

Finally, if you have followed the scam through to this stage, the scammer will ring back at a pre-agreed time and explain that they will need you to post the cash to their security department for safekeeping until the investigation is completed. They will provide you with a postal address and insist on you packing the cash in a particular way. This may involve initially wrapping it in foil to protect it from detection, followed by more standard brown paper or a padded envelope.

THE TELLS

Out-of-the-blue approach.

Pressure, impression of urgency.

Unusual actions (withdrawing large amounts of money as cash).

Isolating from sources of trust ('Do not speak to family members or friends about this').

Requests for excessive personal information.

< 71 >

THE ONLINE SHOPPING SCAM

The most ubiquitous version of this scam relates to online shopping giant Amazon. This is no fault of Amazon themselves, it is simply a very good 'in' for scammers dealing with customers in the UK or US because almost everyone has an Amazon account. What this means is that it gives the vast majority of us a reason to engage with the phone call rather than hang up before the scam has even begun. The last thing a scammer wants is to waste time and money by missing out on a potential victim because they made an approach that was simply too niche.

It will begin in one of two ways: you receive a call from a robotic voice explaining either that you have been charged an annual subscription fee for your online shopping account or that there have been suspicious transactions on your account. If you do not wish to continue your subscription/want to cancel the suspicious transactions, you must press 1 to speak to customer support. If you do so, you will be taken on one of two routes:

Variation 1 – Subscription Refund

In order for you to receive your refund for your supposed annual subscription, you'll be told that you must fill out an online form for which the scammer will provide the web address. It will be dressed up to look like an official document related to the company, but it is actually an information-gathering exercise designed to part you with your banking information.

Before you fill in the form, they'll request you download a remote access app or piece of software for your device in order to 'establish a connection to our secure server'. Should you question this, they will likely explain that it is necessary to help you through the process of receiving your refund but that it will not allow them to see or control your device.

< 72 >

The reality is that this allows the scammer to see your device's screen if you share your device's unique ID number when requested and may also let them control your device, should you pass through some security steps designed to relinquish control.

Once you have completed the form, which includes filling in banking information for the account you wish to receive the refund into, you will be instructed to check your online banking app (if you have one) to see if your refund has arrived. It hasn't, because you were never due a refund. This is a chance for the scammer to see the contents of your bank account, because they have remote access.

Some online banking apps, however, now block remote access, which will lead to the scammer seeing only a blank screen for your device when you log in. If this is the case with your bank, the scammer's next step will be to ask you to open your device's calculator. They will explain that you need to enter the total amount in your account, minus the cost of the annual subscription for which you are expecting a refund so you can see what your balance should be once the refund is received. Again, this is solely intended to allow the scammer to know exactly how much money is in your account.

They will also ask you to add in balances of other accounts to this if you have savings accounts etc., because what they really want to discover from this process is this: whether or not you have more than £1,000 in total that they can steal from you. The vast majority of scammers will not bother with you if your accounts contain less than this amount – it is not worth the time it takes them to steal. If you do have less than £1,000, they will likely hang up at this point or simply state that they can 'fix the problem' from their end.

Should the scam proceed, the scammer will explain that they'll need to pass you on to a more senior colleague to fix the failure of the refund to appear. There are a couple of variations again on what potentially comes next.

< 73 >

The first involves this senior colleague explaining that in order to receive your refund, as it has not worked through your online banking, they will use a digital banking or payment app. This will involve you downloading the application of a digital bank which operates in the UK or US. You will need to go through the process of setting up an account, which can be quite involved.

It will likely insist that you take a selfie and submit some form of photo ID. They will justify this by explaining that if you want your refund in this method, you need to accept that you have to prove who you are to their company. Once the banking app account has been created, they will explain that in order to receive your refund you need to use the 'Add Money' function of the app.

When this is clicked on, the app will request details of the account you wish to add the money from – the scammer will tell you to put in your own, because that's where you want to add the money. The reality is that by doing this, you will be adding money from your own account into this newly created banking app.

At this point, the scammer will ask you to set up a transfer and enter the details of the sending account, which they claim is your online shopping company's. Should you do as they ask and send to the account details they request you to enter, instead of appearing in your own original account, your money will be gone.

The second method works like this: the senior manager will start distracting you with tasks such as taking down long case reference numbers or verifying yourself by giving your full email address, home address, date of birth and similar. As you do that, they will use their access to your device to edit your online banking account to appear as if you have been refunded far too much money. If you were 'due' £79.99, they might, for example, make it appear that you have been refunded £7,999. This is done using the code which makes your online banking appear as it does – it is worryingly easy to edit if you know how.

< 74 >

They will then explain that you need to send the difference back to the online shopping company. They will provide a mule account for you to transfer the money to, often suggesting that the refund is their error and if you don't do it, they could lose their job. If you do this, you will never hear from 'customer support' nor see your money again.

Variation 2 – Suspicious Transactions

Here, the scammer will explain that there have been transactions attempted on your account which they do not believe were done by you. This is not true, but they're going to try to prove it to you.

Firstly, they will ask you to check your text messages for a six-digit passcode sent by your online shopping company, to prove their legitimacy. They will likely reference the number of scams going around to emphasize how important this step is before asking for the email address you use to log in to your account. There is indeed a text there – but it's been generated by the scammers, who have entered your number or email address into the online shopping company's website and requested a password reset.

This has led to your actual online shopping company automatically sending out a six-figure one-time passcode, or OTP, intended just for you to be able to reset your password. These codes will always come with a warning not to share them – but the scammer will say that is intended for anyone outside the company; it's fine to share it with the company's employees. This is absolutely not true, no OTP should ever be shared with anyone.

If you do share this code with the scammer, they will be able to reset your password from their end and access your account from wherever they are. They will start adding expensive items to your online shopping basket to make their tale more convincing. They will then suggest that you look at your account yourself (even though they've changed

< 75 >

the password, this doesn't log you out, so you'll still be able to see your account) and sure enough, you'll see items you've never placed in your basket. Suddenly their story of unsolicited transactions on your account appears incredibly legitimate.

Now the scammer will explain that you need to download remote access software (as above), using the same reasons to justify the need for this. They will coach you to delete payment methods from your account to protect yourself, but this is just window dressing designed to make you believe that they are indeed on your side. It also gives them the opportunity to steal more of your data – as you delete stored cards from your account, with remote access they will be able to take pictures of your personal information for later use. What they really want is to gain your trust enough to persuade you to open up your online banking.

When you do so, they will either take the refund approach explained above, suggesting that the expensive items in your basket are currently 'blocked' and that you need to request a refund, or they will try to explain that in order to protect your money, you need to move it to what they call a 'safe account'. This will involve you transferring money, most likely to what they say is a bank account set up by your online shopping company, intended to provide safe haven for the funds of customers who have had their accounts hacked, as they claim yours has been. They will request you to transfer the total amount of money in your affected accounts here for safekeeping until they can secure your online shopping account again. Should you go through with this request, you will simply be transferring your funds into mule accounts controlled by the scammers.

< 76 >

THE TELLS

Out-of-the-blue approach.

One-time passcode sharing (never do this).

Pressure, impression of urgency.

Unusual actions (moving around large amounts
of money, sharing one-time passcodes).

THE MOBILE PHONE COMPANY SCAM

This is another scam that relies heavily upon the sharing of one-time passcodes as a deciding factor. It will begin, as so many do, with a phone call appearing to come out of the blue from your mobile phone network. The caller will often immediately advertise the prospect of a 'lure', essentially the bait on the fishing rod of their scam, something which might sound very appealing to you as a customer. They may begin with an opening line like this: 'We're calling all our valued customers to let them know that we're offering them a 33 per cent discount on their bills/an upgraded phone free of charge/six months of free data.' The next step will be to suggest that in order to receive this attractive offer, all you need to do is read out what they claim is a promotional code they are going to send you by text message. The reality is that the caller will have entered your mobile number into your mobile provider's website, and requested a password reset. The one-time passcode for your account, to be able to reset the password, is what will arrive in your inbox.

Should you read this code to them as requested, the scammer

< 77 >

will be able to log into your account from their end and reset the password to one of their choosing. With access to your account, and all the details it contains, it will be considerably easier for the scammer to make you believe they are indeed your mobile phone provider. At this point, to dress the windows a little, they might run through security questions with you. This will be possible because they can see the account information your mobile provider holds – they are logged into your account, after all. In asking you to confirm the email address or home address related to your account, or what your last monthly bill was, they will further convince you that they are indeed your provider.

Now comes the incredibly devious part. With access to your account, which likely has payment information already stored, they will start changing the contact details associated. They will set up a new email address to communicate with your provider which is similar to your real address, all while keeping you occupied on the phone by discussing aspects of your current deal or asking you to confirm information about yourself.

Once this process is complete, they will get down to the nuts and bolts of the scam – ordering new devices in your name. Searching your mobile provider's shop for the highest value devices that can be delivered as quickly as possible, they will put in purchases for new mobiles or tablets to be delivered to your home address. You will not receive notification or confirmation of these purchases immediately, unless you use online banking and have payment notifications turned on, because they have already changed the email address associated with your account. As such, confirmation of the deals will go to their new email.

With their items bought, they will end the call by congratulating you on your newly reduced bills, or newly upgraded phone, or new package, confirming the lesser amount you'll be paying or the

< 78 >

value of the thing you just got for free. In the days that follow, the scammers will track the delivery of their purchased items to your home. As soon as they know they've arrived, they will be on the phone to you again.

In this second phone call, a 'manager', who is in fact the group's top-performing closer, will call you to explain that there has in fact been a terrible mistake. They will apologize profusely, but they have sent you some items in error, which will need to be returned to the warehouse. If they promised you an upgraded phone, they will claim that it's on its way but these first items are a mistake. They will offer to text you a postage label to be used to return the items. This will arrive in your inbox and the closer will coach you on exactly how to use it – simply print it and affix to the package of items to be returned to the warehouse. If you have noticed the money for these items has already left your account, they will claim that you will receive your refund in the coming days and apologize again for the inconvenience. The postage label will be prepaid, so all you need to do is drop the package at the post office.

Should you go through with this, you will have just sent thousands of pounds' worth of devices, paid for in your name, to what is in fact not a warehouse but a mule address used by the scammers. Soon enough, the brand-new phones and tablets you paid for will be for sale in one of their shops, wherever they might be in the world.

You will be left picking up the pieces, because the consequences of this scam are extremely problematic. Proving to your mobile provider that you did not simply take the devices and sell them on yourself is virtually impossible, meaning getting your money back can be a protracted process. In the meantime, you may even be left in debt.

THE TELLS

Out-of-the-blue approach.

One-time passcode sharing (never do this).

The lure (an attractive offer to tempt you to stay on the line).

Requests for excessive personal information.

THE TECH SUPPORT SCAM (AKA BLUE SCREEN OF DEATH/BSOD SCAM)

Sometimes the old ways are the best ways, and in the world of scams that also rings true. This particular scam variant has been around since the earliest days of the internet and continues today with numerous variations.

If you are not familiar with the 'blue screen of death' (BSOD), it's a phrase which relates to what happens when your Windows-operating computer experiences a system crash. Essentially, something so bad has happened that the device can't continue to operate safely. It can be a very worrying sight, especially if it is not immediately clear what action you might take to fix the issue.

Scammers have capitalized on this panic-inducing screen by taking the visual grammar of the BSOD and, with a bit of crafty computer know-how, making their own versions to satisfy their needs. Although it might sound as if this is more of an online attack, perhaps surprisingly most BSOD scams take place during phone calls.

The scam will begin with what appears to be a blue screen of death failure on your computer. This will likely occur while you're browsing

< 80 >

the internet and appear as a window, not the entire screen. The window element is important here: a real BSOD will take up the entirety of your computer's screen and leave you no option but to follow the instructions on it. A scam BSOD will likely appear as a new window within your internet browser itself. There are rare occasions when the scam BSOD will take up the whole screen, but this requires more complicated work by the scammer.

The scam BSOD will, via some clever programming, appear to freeze your computer's cursor, making it seemingly impossible for you to control the screen using the mouse or trackpad. It will likely also be programmed to play an alarming noise, should you have speakers or headphones. All this is intended to set you off in a panic – wondering what on earth has happened and what you can do to fix it.

The scam BSOD has the answer: it will explain that your computer has suffered a critical error, or that you have somehow obtained what is known as a trojan virus (the most serious kind of virus, essentially a hidden virus which can take over your device) due to your use of the internet. It will suggest in the text that you must immediately call 'Microsoft Support' on a number listed on the screen.

Should you call the number, you will be put through to a scammer posing as a Microsoft engineer, who claims that they will be able to help you fix this issue. One of the first things they will likely ask is exactly what you were doing online which caused this error to appear – their hope being that you will be forced to reveal that you were doing something embarrassing. Many BSOD scams originate on websites with (entirely legal) pornographic content or with slightly legally 'grey' status, like selling incredibly cheap items, or resulting from misspellings of the address of major sites.

Should they catch you doing something which might be a touch embarrassing, the scammer will immediately capitalize on this, shaming

< 81 >

you for your actions and explaining that in order to fix this issue of your own foolish creation, you will need their help. When it comes to the misspelling variation they will again lay the blame at your door if possible by asking if you can check the name of the website you typed in for typos, and should you find one they will explain that hackers use these to break into individual computers.

Having created the idea that your own foolishness has led you to this problem, they will now attempt to build trust, reassuring you that they are in fact the only person who can get you out of the difficult situation you find yourself in. Built into this reassurance will be threats – if you don't go through with it, you could lose everything on your computer to hackers. This is obviously a very frightening thing to hear and puts you exactly where the scammers want you: in a state of panic, outside your rational mind and ready to do whatever they ask.

The most likely next step will be the request that you install a remote access application on your device. This will allow the scammer to 'fix' your problem for you and guide you through the rest of their scam. Once you have their remote access of choice installed, you will be requested to read out your device's ID number (usually a nine-digit number assigned when you install the remote access) and then accept the incoming connection request the scammer makes using your device's ID.

Should you do this, you are granting the scammer access to see your screen, and with a few more security boxes ticked to control the device on your behalf. This is a very dangerous position to be in because the scam can go a number of ways from here. The most common is that the scammer will explain that to fix your problem you will need to pay a fee (usually in the region of £200 or $300) to install software to remove the error.

In order to make you feel that they have performed actions which are worthy of payment, they will likely use aspects of Windows computers which are not familiar to the average user. For example, opening a black

< 82 >

background, white text window called CMD.exe or Command Prompt, which is intended to be used by IT professionals. It allows the entering of text-based commands which then result in the device performing certain actions.

If you are the average Windows computer user, it's highly unlikely you will have seen this before or know what it is. This is perfect for the scammer, who can use their informational advantage to claim that the commands they enter result in various responses which should be of concern to you. The reality is that these will all be standard responses and the information the scammer claims it shows in fact have entirely different (and totally normal) meanings.

After some work on this the scammers will usually insist on taking payment for their 'fix' by means which are a bit of a giveaway, because they might seem strange as a means of paying a legitimate organization, like using gift cards or cryptocurrency. This is because they will not want the transaction to be traceable in any way. Cryptocurrency can be difficult to trace and once a gift card voucher code is read out to a scammer, it is effectively cash.

Should you complete payment, you will have been defrauded for a non-existent issue and paid for a non-existent service. It is also highly likely that in the process of controlling your device, the scammers will install malware (software like an application for your computer, which has bad intentions), which will lead to you receiving more BSODs in future and the scammers being able to try to repeat the scam.

The most crucial piece of advice should you encounter a BSOD when browsing the internet is this: should the BSOD appear to freeze your device and make you unable to control it using the cursor with your mouse or trackpad, there are two simple fixes.

The first is to use three keyboard buttons in combination – Control, Alt and Delete. Pressing these three buttons simultaneously will either take your device to the lock screen immediately, showing the Windows

< 83 >

icon and various options including restart, shut down and start Task Manager, or simply start Task Manager straight away.

Task Manager is a means by which you can shut down or cancel processes currently running on your Windows computer, so once this has started you should be able to use the mouse or trackpad again. Within the Task Manager window you will see a list of the programmes currently running on your device, select your internet browser, or whatever it was you were using when you encountered the BSOD, and right-click on it. This will give you the option to 'end process' or similar.

Once that is done, the BSOD window will disappear and you will again be able to use your device freely. The quicker and easier option is simply to shut down your device by holding the power button for ten seconds (known as the 'kill switch') before restarting it. If you were in the middle of work which was unsaved, this can, however, lead to data loss, so be careful using it as an option.

THE TELLS

Pressure, impression of urgency.

Shame and blame (making you feel embarrassed or ashamed of your actions).

Unusual payment methods (gift cards, cryptocurrency, international or bank transfer).

Informational advantage abuse (claiming to know something you cannot verify).

< 84 >

THE INTERNET PROVIDER SCAM

The internet is obviously a hugely important tool to all of us, particularly in the post-COVID world of remote working. As such, anything which threatens our connection is going to be a big concern. This particular scam often rears its head in the UK during periods of extreme weather, like winter storm season.

Why would an internet provider scam become more common during a time of bad weather? Because it's another brilliant 'in' for the scammers, who you can bet follow news events globally like hawks. It gives them the perfect opening line: 'Hi, I'm calling from your internet provider. I understand the bad weather has meant you've been having some issues with your connection?'

In many cases not only will this be genuinely true for the potential victim on the other end, but even if it isn't, during a time of severe weather it sounds all the more plausible. During periods of calmer climate, the scammer will simply tone it down to something equally ubiquitous, which could be a complaint about the speed of the connection or it dropping in and out. It's a classic example of informational advantage because the reality is this: the vast majority of us have absolutely no idea how broadband wireless internet works. If you asked 100 people in the street, you might get a vaguely plausible explanation from one of them. It is just part of the accepted magic of the modern world. That is a beautiful position for a scammer, who is very comfortable weaponizing that information imbalance against you.

Assuming you answer positively that yes, you have been having some trouble with your connection, the scammer will possibly ask you to go and find your router box. This is the device, located somewhere in your home, which represents the source of the internet. It will be plugged into a phone socket and have several lights on the front, usually three or four. At most times, all of these will be

< 85 >

green. They may blink, and some may turn orange or red if the connection drops.

The scammer will explain that if any of your lights are blinking, it suggests there is an issue with your connection (this is simply not true) which requires further investigation. They are there to help you get it sorted. The start of this will be a request to sit down at the computer you use the most at home.

There are an array of tricks the scammer will use here to deceive you into believing that there is indeed an issue with your internet connection. One of the first of these if you are using a Windows device might be to use CMD.exe or Command Prompt, in a similar way to the BSOD scam. The scammer here will likely use a command that shows the number of connections to your computer. This is designed to concern you that someone is hacking into your device and abusing your connection, either using it for themselves and slowing down your speeds, or because they are stealing your data. Even if your device shows multiple connections, this is nothing to be concerned with; it is just the normal running of a computer connected to the internet and various websites around the world.

An alternative ruse to achieve the same result might be for the scammer to suggest you Google a specific phrase: 'What is my 1p address 66.249'. The seemingly odd phrase is a corruption of 'IP address' intended to throw you off the scent. Were you to Google 'what is my IP address', you would receive a result confirming your genuine IP address, which is your location in the world according to your internet connection. But by making you search for this corruption instead, they will take you to a specific site: https://www.ipaddress.my/66.249.81.46

At this website, what you will see are the results for the IP address 66.249.81.46. This is Google's server in Mountain View, California. It has nothing to do with your location, nor any hackers trying to gain access to your connection – but that's what the scammer will

< 86 >

say. They will claim that the fact that this search gave you that result shows someone in Mountain View, California, is trying to access your device.

By this point you are likely to be very concerned that there are people with bad intentions accessing your internet connection. The internet provider impersonating scammer will use that opportunity to take things up a notch, either going down the route of the tech support scammer and trying to charge you for unnecessary work on your computer, or worse, trying to persuade you to download a remote access app so they can fix the problem.

With you in a panic and as such in the palm of their hands, relinquishing control of your device and allowing the scammer to take control themselves seems perfectly sensible – but at this point the scammer's professional demeanour will drop. If you do indeed give them control, with nowhere else to go to potentially access your money, they will start changing passwords on your device and deleting data. You won't be able to stop them because they will already have requested permission, via the remote access app, for full control of your computer. They will threaten that unless you pay them money, they will delete everything on your device and make it unusable, effectively turning it into junk and leaving you no choice but to buy a new one. Your best course of action in this situation is to turn off your device entirely – holding down the power button for ten seconds will do the trick; it's known as the 'kill switch' and will turn it off whatever the situation. At that point, your best bet is to contact an IT professional who can attend in person to help you out.

< 87 >

THE TELLS

Out-of-the-blue approach.

Informational advantage abuse.

Unusual actions (downloading remote access software).

THE ARREST WARRANT SCAM

This is arguably the most frightening of the phone scams you might encounter, and when it works it can be truly devastating, both emotionally and financially. As with so many of these phone scams, there are multiple variations in use due to the large number of call centres attempting it, each tailoring it and tweaking it to their own tastes.

The basic premise is this: a call out of the blue, possibly a robocall, possibly a cold-calling person speaking to you immediately, explaining there is a warrant for your arrest and you should press 1 to discuss it with the court service. In the UK, this has been done using a spoofed phone number which actually related back to the highest court of appeal in the UK, the Supreme Court, making it doubly convincing.

What this scam also allows is the scammer to speak to you in an incredibly aggressive way, given the position it puts you in from the start. You are essentially on the defensive from the moment that you answer the call and the scammer will know that, using their tone of voice and accusations to wrong-foot you and put you outside of your rational mind immediately.

When you answer the phone and have been told there is an outstanding warrant for your arrest, the scammer will ask you to

< 88 >

confirm your name, date of birth and current address. Once you have done this, they will explain that unfortunately, bank accounts bearing your name have been used in serious criminal activity, such as people trafficking, drug trafficking and weapons purchases. As such, the police have issued a warrant for your arrest. They will go on to explain that the investigation is a matter for you and you alone, and should you speak to friends or family about it, you will potentially affect the integrity of the police's investigation into the criminals concerned. As such, it is imperative that you keep this call to yourself and do not share information about it with anyone.

Should you wish to resolve this situation and avoid arrest, you will need to go through an ID-verification process with the caller to prove who you are. At this point they may request further personal information about you beyond what they already have, like your known addresses for the past five years, marital status, home ownership status etc., as part of what they call asset declaration. This is just a data-gathering exercise. It allows the scammers to build a profile of you with a high level of detail, which they will then be able to sell on to other call centres.

At this point in the call, the scammer will do their utmost to make sure you are terrified. The rebuttals used in this scam (the responses to any questions or doubts you may have) are some of the cruellest and most brutal in any phone scam. Expressing doubt in what they are saying to you will simply result in them suggesting it is fine to end the call but should you do so, you can expect the police to arrive at your property within the next twenty-four hours to arrest you. It is likely they will also list the appalling consequences of this, including the potential prison sentence you face, should you be found guilty.

Having put you in this position of profound terror, the scammer will reveal that there are two options available to you. The first is to go to trial and face the prospect of whatever sentence is decided, should you

< 89 >

be found guilty. They will explain that if you take this option, there will possibly be legal fees involved, as you will need a lawyer. But the second, considerably cheaper, option is what they may call 'alternative dispute resolution', or ADR.

They will claim that should you be willing to go down this ADR route, it will be looked upon very well by the court and your case will be resolved much more quickly. All that is required is the immediate payment of a large amount of money, as a form of bail, to offset the arrest warrant. This is all total nonsense and absolutely nothing to do with how the legal system works. It is worth noting at this point that the last thing the police would do if they had an arrest warrant out for you is have someone call and tell you about it.

It will be explained that you either need to transfer funds to the investigating department's account to cover the costs, or to pay by some other means like gift cards. If it is the latter and you question this method, they will justify it by explaining it is a quick and widely available way of transferring money to them.

At this point in the call, they may offer you a number of methods to prove that they are serious and are who they say they are, should you be concerned about the legitimacy of what you're hearing. One method is to suggest that they can have the local police station call you – where they will genuinely spoof the number of a nearby police station and ring you using it. Another is to spoof a number related to another government authority and have another person say that the call is legitimate from that line. Either way, these two separate approaches apparently from government officials are highly likely to get you over the line.

Should you transfer any money, the call will be ended almost immediately.

< 90 >

THE TELLS

Out-of-the-blue approach.

Pressure, impression of urgency.

Shame and blame (making you feel embarrassed
or ashamed of your actions).

Unusual actions (moving around large amounts of money).

Isolating from sources of trust ('Do not speak to
family members or friends about this').

Unusual payment methods (gift cards, cryptocurrency,
international or bank transfer).

Requests for excessive personal information.

THE UNPAID TAX SCAM

Peaking in February and May every year in the UK, this scam is highly effective in parting individuals with substantial sums in short order. It will usually start with a robocall explaining you have unpaid tax in your name and need to press 1 to speak to a caseworker to avoid being fined. Some even more threatening versions might suggest the suspension of your National Insurance number in the UK, or Social Security number in the US, and the seizure of your assets. This is obviously a very worrying thing to hear and an excellent incentive to press 1 and immediately get put through to a scammer. Should you begin speaking to the caseworker, they will start by claiming to work for the tax authority in

< 91 >

your country, HM Revenue and Customs in the UK or the Internal Revenue Service (IRS) in the US. Their manner will be extremely professional and calm, attempting to maintain the usual neutral tone of someone working for a government organization.

They will ask you to share some details about your situation, to allow them to understand your case. This will include identifying information like your name, date of birth and home address, as well as information about your tax set-up – are you freelance, do you pay tax as you earn (PAYE) in the UK? It is important to remember that any genuine organization should not need to ask you for all this information; they would likely just ask one or two questions to confirm who you are. Your information, once handed to scammers, is almost as valuable as the money to be made from the scam, as it allows them to sell on your data to the next group at a high price. The better the quality of data, the more the next group will be willing to pay for it.

All this is also helpful for them in knowing what to say when they explain later in the call that unfortunately (if you're freelance or in the US) you have miscalculated on your taxes for the previous year. If you pay as you earn in the UK, they will explain that there has been an issue with your employer's payments, resulting in underpayment, which you must address. They will suggest that you are ultimately responsible for your tax affairs being in order, even if the payments are supposed to be automatically deducted from your salary.

In order to solve this problem, the only solution is to pay immediately by money transfer. It is unlikely that they will accept card payment (this is all too easy for you to dispute with your bank), so they will insist on a direct bank transfer in the UK or the use of a transfer app in the US, where direct bank transfer is not possible without one.

Should you go ahead with this transaction, it might be that the scammers get greedy and start attempting to extract more money from you, citing advance payments on next year's tax to offset future amounts

< 92 >

owed ahead of time. Once you have paid up, you will likely be thanked for settling the outstanding amount and told that the case is now closed and no further action necessary.

THE TELLS

Out-of-the-blue approach.

Pressure, impression of urgency.

Shame and blame (making you feel embarrassed or ashamed of your actions).

Isolating from sources of trust ('Do not speak to family members or friends about this').

Unusual payment methods (gift cards, cryptocurrency, international or bank transfer).

Requests for excessive personal information.

POLICE IMPERSONATION SCAMS

This is another cold call that relies on causing you instant alarm and distress to work but which also takes advantage of the way in which some landline phones function. There are variations on the way it works or what approach is taken by the scammers using this, in terms of who they may choose to impersonate, but the umbrella term used to describe these is a 'no hang-up' scam.

The police impersonation version is arguably the most frightening. It

< 93 >

will likely start with a call from a scammer impersonating your bank's fraud department. They will explain that there have been suspicious transactions on your card that day and that they have been in touch with the police. They will begin by asking you for personal and banking information to verify who you are.

Should you act at all suspicious, they will offer to put you in touch with the local police station who are dealing with the situation related to your card. They will explain that someone is already in custody and there is an officer assigned to your case, giving a name and a badge number. They will also give the actual direct line of a police station near to you if such a thing exists, suggesting that you call them immediately to verify what they are saying. They also leave a number to reach them again.

Crucially, after saying goodbye the scammer will stay on the line, in silence. Many older models of landline phones, even if you yourself believe you have ended the call, will not disconnect if the other caller stays on the line. They will wait in silence as you dial the number for your local police station – and when you're done, they will play the sound of ringing down the phone.

A different scammer answers, posing as the investigating police officer on your case. They explain that yes, what your bank's fraud department told you was correct. Someone is in fact in custody, having been caught using your card in various shops. They will also suggest that you may need to come down to the station at some point to give evidence. They end the call, telling you to speak to your bank again and have new cards issued, accounts set up and even, to be totally safe, to consider moving any money you have in the account related to that card.

Using the number given to you by the first scammer, you call them back, now believing you have had verification from a police officer both of the fact that they are your bank and that they are telling the truth. You've also had some ideas about action to take seeded in your mind – moving money. The scammer answers and proceeds with their discussion of your

< 94 >

situation, suggesting they send out new cards to you straight away. But, crucially, they also believe it to be wise to move your money from your current account associated with the card, to protect it. Of course, as per the bank impersonation scam, they will likely suggest moving it to a 'safe account' controlled by the bank's fraud department. Should you do so, it will be the last you hear of this situation ever again, and likely the last you see of that money.

THE TELLS

Out-of-the-blue approach.

Pressure, impression of urgency.

Unusual actions (moving around large amounts of money, sharing one-time passcodes).

THE LOAN SCAM

Essentially a complex variation of advanced fee fraud, this is one of the most deviously put together scams around and relies on two extremely potent tools to work. The first is a huge amount of your personal information and the second is a very attractive lure. It is very effective and near-impossible to sniff out as a scam, but thankfully it only applies to a smaller group of people – those applying for a personal loan.

The nature of the loan business across the world is that if you need a personal loan, it is probably going to be found for you using a broker. These are essentially middlemen companies whose job is to find you the best loan for your needs in return for a small percentage of it as a fee.

< 95 >

What this means is that many of those needing a personal loan apply through a brokerage website.

Perhaps unsurprisingly, scammers have realized this and created scam brokerage websites that are extremely difficult to tell from the real thing, often exact copies of genuine brokerages with a few very minor changes made. Should you apply for a loan through a scam brokerage website, you will need to submit a large amount of personal information, as you would when applying on a genuine website. This will include your name, phone numbers, date of birth, address, address history, bank, possibly account numbers and sort codes (to have money paid into), National Insurance number (or equivalent outside the UK), whether you have any other loans in your name (like a car lease) or credit card debt, what your credit rating is, whether you own your home, have a mortgage, or rent, your monthly income and also the reason you want the loan.

Unfortunately, in the hands of a scammer, that is extremely powerful information. Once submitted to a scam brokerage website and with your detailed personal information now in their hands, you will likely receive a call not long afterwards from someone claiming to represent a legitimate large-scale loan company. Now comes the lure – the scammers will congratulate you that your loan has been approved and they just need to confirm some information with you first.

They will then run through a lot of the information you have just submitted online, which will add to their legitimacy in your eyes as they will be feeding information back to you which you have only just submitted yourself. Once this process is complete, they will explain that they need to put you through to a loan manager to finalize the transaction and that the money will arrive in your account that same day.

You'll be passed on to another scammer, who will again congratulate you and tell you that your personal loan is ready to be sent over. The last step that needs to be taken is one of two things: you must either pass a credit check or insure your loan. If they say the former, they

< 96 >

will briefly place you on hold and then explain that unfortunately your credit rating is not good enough, so you will need to pay a small fee to secure the loan. This might be as little as £50 or as much as £500, depending on what they think they can get away with. Should they say that you need to insure the loan, they will justify this by referring to genuine forms of (extremely controversial in the UK) payment insurance like payment protection insurance (PPI). They will remind you that your loan will arrive the same day if you go ahead. Either way, their only goal will be to get you to perform a bank transfer of cash into an account they claim is associated with their business. Should you pay, they will end the call, explaining that your loan will arrive shortly.

This is a particularly nightmarish type of scam to work out, purely because of how well it fits into your genuine personal circumstances and because of the amount of detailed personal information the scammers will have on you. It is worth mentioning here that the only way to be sure it is a scam is to tell the caller you're going to hang up and call back whatever company they represent on a number you have for them.

THE TELLS

Unusual payment methods (gift cards, cryptocurrency, international or bank transfer).

The lure (an attractive offer to tempt you to stay on the line).

Advance fee (a small upfront payment to secure a future benefit, e.g. money).

< 97 >

THE WHITE GOODS INSURANCE SCAM

This scam, which has broadly been run from the south coast of the UK for the past decade or more, focuses on the sale of nonsense, non-existent insurance products for white goods, such as dryers, washing machines and boilers. It might also be known as a home appliance cover scam.

It will begin with a cold call from a call centre agent, explaining that they believe your insurance on some of the white goods in your home may be about to lapse. They may even claim to represent major insurance companies or give a company name that sounds as if it could come under the umbrella of a known insurance company. They will go on to suggest that should you wish to renew it, they can help. What they do not explain is that they are calling from a private company with absolutely nothing to do with your insurer at all – it is just an attempt to trick you.

Should you proceed with the conversation, they will begin suggesting that in order to renew, they will need to confirm your bank details. They do not actually know them, this is purely an attempt to get you to reveal them. By sharing your account number and sort code, you are in fact setting them up for the first part of their scam – bogus direct debits. The agent will then explain that your insurance renewal will cost a certain amount and that payment will need to be taken over the phone using your card details.

While you are doing this, they will be setting up various other payments to go out once your phone call is complete, all for imaginary products and services you have not agreed to. The worst thing about this scam is that in many cases it has been found that the companies engaging in this practice are not selling any viable form of insurance, they are simply taking payment for a product that does not exist. As such, they never send paperwork related to the sale or any kind of insurance documentation like a cover note. The victims of this scam then find themselves in a very difficult position if something does go

< 98 >

wrong with their appliance: they are not only unable to find details on their insurance, they are stuck with an appliance they believe they have been paying insurance on and which they may well not be able to afford to fix themselves.

THE TELLS

Out-of-the-blue approach.

Requests for excessive personal information.

Advance fee (a small upfront payment to secure a future benefit, e.g. money).

THE HOME REPAIRS SCAM

This cold call scam has become increasingly popular in the past few years, particularly targeting the UK, where issues of disrepair and poor housing quality are extremely common. The scammer calling will state that they are from the 'housing repair team', or even 'your local authority', and go ahead with asking you if you are facing any issues of disrepair in your home. They will even list some appropriate issues that you may consider you have, such as damp, mould, leaks and lack of heating or hot water.

Should you respond positively, they will begin requesting information about your property status – do you rent your home? If so, is it from a private landlord, the local council or a housing association? If you explain that you own the property, they will end the call by explaining this service is only for those renting property – obviously a huge proportion of the population, particularly in the UK.

< 99 >

Next, the scammer will ask you to go through your personal information, including phone numbers, email address, home address, the number of years you have lived at the property, how much you pay in rent and all the details related to the disrepair you are dealing with in your home. They will often encourage you to consider other aspects of disrepair beyond those which come immediately to mind, asking about the condition of other rooms and parts of the property you may not have considered. At the end of this process, the scammer will thank you for your time and tell you that a member of the housing repair team will be in touch shortly.

So where is the scam?

This call is known as 'claim farming', the scammer's sole intention being to get details from you which will be sufficient for them to sell on to a legal firm, who will then pester you with calls and messages about your possible claim against your landlord for failure to repair your property to an appropriate standard. It is one of an increasing number of scams that are not interested in your money at all – they are interested in the most modern form of currency, your data.

The buying and selling of our data is going to become an increasingly profitable outlet for scammers, not least because so many of us allow it to flow from us freely without necessarily realizing the value it has, every time we sign up for a new account online or download an app without bothering to read the terms and conditions.

THE TELLS

Out-of-the-blue approach.

Requests for excessive personal information.

< 100 >

PENSION SCAMS

Arguably deserving of an entire chapter of their own, pension scams are notorious for a number of reasons: the unbelievable damage they can cause financially, the way they can go unnoticed sometimes even for years and the appalling emotional burden on families who suffer them. The cost-of-living crisis affecting the world has made this problem far worse also, as many families look to release cash from pension pots early to help with their increased day-to-day costs.

From a phone call perspective, thankfully the UK government has taken some substantial action against pension scams – cold-calling with financial products to sell is outright illegal in the UK and cold calls relating to pension advice have been banned since 2019. If you do receive a call of that nature, you can easily discount it immediately as a scam. As ever, the scammers have their tricksy ways around whatever the authorities attempt to do to stop them, and with pension scams these are no different.

Many pension scams will start with an out-of-the-blue call offering you something along the lines of 'free pension advice', claiming they do not have anything to sell and as such are doing nothing wrong at all. The reality is that professional advice of any kind does tend to cost you money, and that is no different when it comes to pensions.

It is very likely that any 'free pension advice' caller will try to get you on the hook early, using specifically targeted phrases like 'early access' and 'guaranteed returns' to get you dreaming of your retirement and financial freedom. They will probably also suggest that the offer they are able to secure for you is only available for a limited time, and that in order to hear more you will need to call somebody else.

This first caller will want to get you to call a second person, whose advice will certainly not be intended to benefit you. The reason for using the second call at all will be to make tracking them down difficult for

< 101 >

the authorities, should you realize what they have done later down the line. Many who have suffered a pension scam do not even notice it has happened for months or even years, the nature of pensions being that we don't touch them until it's possible to withdraw our money, and certainly don't check the balance regularly.

In the second call, you will be told that by moving your pension to a more profitable product, you will see far better returns. In order to enact this process, you'll need to sign various forms passing over permission to deal with your pension to this new adviser. Unfortunately, if you go through with this, you could face a number of quite dramatic consequences.

First of all, early release of pensions can result in tax penalties, so should this be what happens you might face a penalty of as much as 60 per cent of the pot. Worse, your scam adviser might steal the pot altogether, leaving you with nothing at all. Some of the more scrupulous advisers of this nature might simply invest it into extremely high-risk products which could potentially see it lose value rather than gain it, and they will charge a handsome fee for their services too.

The most important thing to remember with absolutely any type of financial advice like this in the UK is at the bare minimum checking that the adviser is from an FCA-regulated firm. The FCA (Financial Conduct Authority) have a list of regulated firms which can be checked on their website. If your adviser is not there – you may have been scammed. If you aren't in the UK, check government websites for your country's resources on where you can obtain legitimate advice on your pension.

If you have indeed been affected by a pension scam like this, you should contact your original pension provider immediately and explain what has happened. They may be able to reverse any transfers of money if you act quickly. If any of the above sounds familiar, don't hesitate.

< 102 >

THE TELLS

Out-of-the-blue approach.

Pressure, impression of urgency.

The lure (an attractive offer to tempt you to stay on the line).

Informational advantage abuse (claiming to know something you cannot verify).

Requests for excessive personal information.

Advance fee (a small upfront payment to secure a future benefit, e.g. money).

THE COMPENSATION SCAM

Have you been injured in an accident or a fall that wasn't your fault?

That phrase will certainly send shivers down the spine of some of you, as you may remember it featuring in a swathe of TV and radio ads over the years, many advertising perfectly legitimate law firms. But scammers have once again taken something from the real world and spun it to their own needs, taking steps into the field of compensation for imagined accidents. This scam will begin with a cold call, most likely a robocall, but with a twist. It may initially appear to sound like a real person you're talking to, friendly, professional, opening with something like: 'Hello, this is X calling Y. I understand you were recently involved in an accident that wasn't your fault, is that correct?'

This is a robocall, but one that has been set up with voice recognition. If you respond in the affirmative, you will be put through to a scammer

< 103 >

immediately. What usually follows will be a very professional-sounding individual ready to hear the terms of your claim and go through some admin with you to sort it out. They promise that should you follow their instructions, you will be highly likely to win compensation.

The initial parts of this will be an information-gathering exercise, designed to obtain as much of your personal data as possible, either to be sold on to another group or used in future scams. Once you have completed their requests regarding registration, they will also go through the process of having you describe the accident that occurred and what injuries or issues you faced as a result. All this is purely window dressing for what is to come. Finally, once you've invested a good amount of your time in the call will come the catch. In order for them to work on your behalf to obtain the compensation, there will be an upfront fee, in the form of a deposit. This is fairly standard practice when appointing a legitimate lawyer. Unfortunately, in this case, if you pay the requested amount, which will again most likely be by bank transfer, although it could involve a card payment, you will be told that your lawyer will be in touch with you shortly, and you will never hear from this group again.

THE TELLS

Out-of-the-blue approach.

Advance fee (a small upfront payment to secure a future benefit, e.g. money).

Requests for excessive personal information.

< 104 >

THE LOFT INSULATION SCAM

This scam may be quite UK-specific, but it's been doing the rounds for a long time and leaves those who fall for it seriously out of pocket. Almost always beginning with a robocall that claims to be from a lung disease-related organization or building standards industry body, the broad brushstrokes are the insistence that your loft insulation is potentially harmful.

This seems like an incredibly niche attack, but it plays on uncertainty in Britain caused by various scandals around loft insulation, including spray foam insulation, which has often been declared unsafe or unsuitable. It also leans on the concern some individuals might have about asbestos, lead and other related products previously used in home building which have subsequently been proven to be harmful to our health. The result is that for those to whom the call has any relevance, should they live in an older house or a home with a loft space or attic, they are immediately put into a slight state of panic – ideal for the scammers.

After the robocall you will be requested to press 1 to speak to a customer support agent for whatever organization they claim to represent. This person will initially explain to you, using entirely bogus science, that the loft insulation in your home has been found to be likely to make you or your family unwell. They will go through various details with you related to your home: the address, the size, the age, the value and the last time it was checked for hazardous materials. This might sound like necessary information to give over, but it is actually just going to provide a solid basis from which the scammer can work out exactly how wealthy you are and how much they can try to take you for. It will also give them a better grounding on which to justify their ridiculous claims about the insulation possibly making you unwell, because they will simply have more detail about your property to spin into believable lies.

With that information in their possession, there are two possible

< 105 >

subsequent approaches. The most brazen is to simply start quoting for the cost of the work, explaining exactly what they charge for a loft the size of yours, when you can expect work to start and how much they will need to be paid upfront. On building work, this could be as much as 50 per cent, which may run into the thousands depending on what they think they can get from you. This will likely then be charged over the phone, either by card or by bank transfer.

The alternative and more professional option here is that they subsequently send someone they claim is a surveyor or one of their specialists to your property to assess what is necessary. Sure enough, somebody will arrive in the days after and take some photographs. They will then attempt to sell you on the work needed in person, often using pressure-selling tactics like time-limited offers to try to get you over the line. Again, payment will likely be made over the phone using card or bank transfer. Whatever method they use, you will have been made to pay for completely unnecessary work without ever having had the chance to get a second opinion.

THE TELLS

Out-of-the-blue approach.

Informational advantage abuse (claiming to know something you cannot verify).

Requests for excessive personal information.

Pressure, impression of urgency.

< 106 >

THE MISSED CALL SCAM

Arguably one of the most intriguing and strange scam types to have emerged in the past decade or so, the missed call scam relies on your own personal curiosity to defraud you. It uses the development of caller ID on smartphones, which enables us to see the number and origin of the person calling us, to pique our interest enough to want to know more.

Also known as a *Wangiri* scam (the Japanese word for 'one ring and cut'), it is an incredibly simple but effective way of making a good amount of money with very minimal effort. Scammers set up a premium rate phone line, of which they are the beneficiary. They then buy up landline phone numbers in exotic, far-off locations, such as lesser-known countries in Africa or remote islands. With these numbers in their possession, they use a robodialler to dial out (the phone device used by large-scale scam call centres to do thousands of robocalls a day), except they never connect any of the calls. In fact, they intentionally call at night, or during working hours, hanging up immediately before anyone has the chance to answer. All the victim will see is a missed call from a very intriguing location.

Many of us will find that our natural curiosity gets the better of us and won't be able to resist calling back to see who it was that phoned us from Guam, St Helena or Djibouti. But here's the thing – if you do it, every single second you spend on that line will cost you. It won't be a huge amount, but enough that if repeated hundreds or even thousands of times, it will be very profitable for our scammers.

The really clever *Wangiri* scammers will add an extra little trick into their arsenal – buying up international numbers which might, at first glance, look like UK mobile numbers or US mobile numbers, depending on where they are calling. For example, if calling the UK, buying up a selection of +7 international codes will potentially trick people into thinking they have missed a call from a UK mobile number, which all

< 107 >

begin with '07'. In doing this, the scammers make more people likely to call their premium rate, international line, simply by virtue of them not realizing they are calling an unusual number.

The key lesson from this one is simple – don't call back any very exotic international numbers you miss a call from, and check the numbers you do miss calls from carefully before you do anything at all.

THE TELLS

Out-of-the-blue approach.

The lure (in this case an intriguing call).

< 108 >

4

Email Scams

Did this email come out of the blue?

Assume it's a scam.

Does it appear to have come from a legitimate source?

Check the sender by clicking or tapping on their name to see their actual email address. It should follow the same formula as the actual company's website e.g. @companyname.com.

Is there a lure or a scare?

Are you being offered a prize or incentive, or is there information in the message intended to cause you panic?

Does the content of the email read like a legitimate corporate communication if it's intended to be one?

Real emails from genuine companies will rarely if ever contain spelling mistakes or poor grammar and would certainly not seek to put you under pressure or feel alarmed.

Thoroughly verify all the information in the email before engaging with it.

Does it contain any information about the company it claims to be from, e.g. address, web address, phone number etc., which can be double-checked using a search engine or by asking a trusted friend or relative?

< 109 >

THE CELEBRITY ENDORSEMENT SCAM

This is an email scam you'll find in almost every single junk folder on the planet. Celebrity endorsement scams, both in our emails and our social media feeds, have become an extremely effective way for scammers to start the process of another scam type.

Using a famous face – sometimes known and trusted with expertise in a certain field related to money, but increasingly as scammers run out of this kind of celebrity just anyone at all – scammers will send out a message claiming something like: 'Nick Stapleton has declared his number one secret to financial freedom, the banks hate him …' There will also be a smiling photo, accompanied by the logo of whatever it is they might be selling.

Nine times out of ten, at the moment, these kind of scams relate to investment in cryptocurrency, or some newly discovered method of investment that is guaranteeing incredible returns for those who dare to try it. The celebrity's endorsements will be peppered throughout the email as they explain how they were sceptical at first but quickly saw amazing returns on their money, how it now allows them total financial freedom and their belief is that everyone deserves to know about it.

Once you reach the end of the article, you will inevitably be invited to click on a link to register your interest, which will involve submitting a small amount of seemingly innocent data like your name, email and mobile number. Still in your mind is the trusted face who has told you this isn't just legitimate, it's brilliant, so this will seem natural. Shortly afterwards you will likely receive a phone call starting the scam. The vast majority of these celebrity endorsements lead to investment scams, which tend to take a shape like this: the scammer will explain that in order to get signed up on their website, you will need a cryptocurrency wallet first. This is just an online place to keep money which you turn into cryptocurrency.

< 110 >

A BRIEF DESCRIPTION OF CRYPTOCURRENCY

Cryptocurrency is a currency which only exists online; it's no different to turning your money into dollars or yen, other than the fact that 'crypto' is designed with cryptography, which makes it near-impossible to counterfeit. It exists on networks of computers across the globe called the blockchain, which form a public record of transactions. All the transactions are encrypted, so even though they are public, they aren't traceable to anyone in particular, just to wallets, which are represented by a collection of numbers and letters.

Transactions made in this way aren't verified by banks, because crypto exists entirely outside of traditional finance networks. You can turn your pounds or dollars into crypto and send crypto to another person's wallet, and your bank will only see that you sent money to a cryptocurrency platform. They will have no idea about where it went after that. In that sense, it's like cash, which is one reason why scammers love it.

With a wallet set up on a cryptocurrency trading platform, the scammer will encourage you to send money to a wallet address they provide, which will get you trading on their site, just like celebrity endorser Nick Stapleton. You can start small just to see that it works. At the same time, you'll be given login details to their website – let's call it www.TradewithNick.com. At Trade with Nick, once you've logged in, you will be looking at what appears to be a functioning website for the buying and selling of cryptocurrency

< 111 >

stocks. Once you've worked out how to use it, with the help of the scammer on the phone, you'll even be able to see your initial investment sat there, let's say £200. At this point the scammer will let you go and tell you to log in again in a few days and see how your TradewithNick investments are doing.

Sure enough, a few days later the promised returns are looking amazing. TradewithNick's site is showing your initial return of £200 as now valued at £500, thanks to their incredibly clever investments in particular cryptocurrencies. You'll even be able to see graphs of it rising and falling. You might start to feel very excited, confident even to put more money in, and your scammer friends won't waste any time getting back on the phone to encourage that. But here's the thing – the entire site, TradewithNick, is fake. It's all smoke and mirrors designed to give you the confidence to send more of your money to that original cryptocurrency wallet, the reality being that every time you do, it isn't being invested at all, it's going in the pockets of the scammers.

A trusted face, and this level of deception giving you such confidence, are a potent combination. It's no surprise that these kinds of scams are some of the most prevalent landing in our email inboxes.

THE TELLS

Out-of-the-blue approach.

The lure (an attractive offer to tempt you).

Unusual payment methods (gift cards, cryptocurrency, international or bank transfer).

Informational advantage abuse (claiming to know something you cannot verify).

< 112 >

THE PRIZE WINNER
(AND A QUICK LESSON IN URLS!)

Absolutely guaranteed, if you were to go to your email's junk folder right now, you would find about six of these emails. They are popular and widely used by scammers all over the world because they work. You will also hear them referred to as 'phishing', which describes fraudulent attempts to get hold of your personal information by deception.

Incredibly simple and incredibly effective, the prize-winner email uses the classic lure technique to draw you in with the prospect of a high-value item, entirely for free. Depending on who the email purports to be from, this can mean a range of items, from a giant toolset to a luxury food processor, a massive television to a voucher for shopping worth hundreds of pounds. To claim your prize, you just need to click on a link and complete a short survey. This survey will take you to a site which seems to be on behalf of whoever the email came from, requesting your responses to relatively mundane questions about your experiences shopping with that company, your habits etc. The questionnaire will have what look like comments underneath it with five-star reviews from other happy customers who have previously filled it out and received their gift. Most likely, there will also be a ticking clock, emphasizing that you've only got six minutes to finish up the survey and claim your gift.

None of this is anything to do with the scam, but it serves a few quite simple psychological purposes: the first is to get you to invest time, so that when you get to the end (and are asked to do what the scammers really want you to do), you're less likely to close the page and give up. The second is just window dressing, making you feel as if this is really the kind of survey a high-street shopping brand might want you to fill out, because it is. The clock also puts you under time pressure and may take you outside your rational mind.

< 113 >

Once you've invested five minutes filling out the form and have completed the survey, you will reach the last page, supposedly the final step before you can claim your prize. It will be a form asking for various pieces of personal information, like your name, address, postcode, email address, phone number – and your card details. Why do they need your card details if it's supposed to be free?

What they failed to mention at the start is that even though your £1,000 new lawnmower is absolutely free, you need to pay the shipping cost of £9. But it's only £9, and for such an expensive item you might as well go for it. From that the scammers don't only get £9 – remember that in the scammer's world, data is almost worth as much as money, and can be worth more. Particularly if it's a scam victim's data which they can sell on to another group. What that means is that those who do fall for these kind of scams often find that only days later, they are suddenly getting phone calls from other scammers with entirely different and sometimes much more serious approaches, which may lead to far greater financial loss. Those second scammers also have a huge advantage – they're starting the scam with a lot of your personal information.

This is the first lesson in the importance of checking the URL (Uniform Resource Locator, internet speak for the website address) when you are about to click any link in an email, text or elsewhere online. The quick way to figure out if it is legit is to use a search engine to find the official website of the company you believe you're dealing with. If the link you've been sent is not a variation on their official site, like the below made-up example, you're in a dangerous spot: www.officialwebsite.com/officiallink.

Somewhat unhelpfully, there is now the possibility to use URL shorteners to cut the length of your web address down to reduce the length of a message. That might make the above look like something different, as follows: Oficlwbs.com/oflik. These can even take an entirely

< 114 >

different look to the original link, which again is quite unhelpful, as follows: Shorturl.com/shrt. Thankfully, you can also check these by searching for a URL checker online and cut and pasting the link into it to see what it actually represents.

THE TELLS

Out-of-the-blue approach.

Pressure, impression of urgency.

The lure (an attractive offer to tempt you).

Advance fee (a small upfront payment to secure a future benefit, e.g. your prizes).

Dodgy URL (the web address is not the official website of the company it claims to be).

THE HONEY TRAP

The idea of the honey trap, essentially the usage of an attractive person to entice the victim into an action they wouldn't normally engage in, isn't anything new. You can trace honey traps right back to the First World War, and they were probably in use before then.

In the early 1900s world of espionage, a honey trap would usually be an attractive young woman, sent to try to seduce a high-ranking government official of a country's enemy, or even a powerful member of its armed forces. The honey trap's job would be to extract 'kompromat', what the Russians call compromising material, to eventually allow

< 115 >

the honey trap's employer to blackmail the victim into giving up vital intelligence or state secrets.

What does this have to do with an email scam? Apply the same logic to an email coming out of the blue, from what appears to be an attractive member of the opposite sex. Inevitably, ninety-nine times out of one hundred this will be a woman, as scammers seem to believe men are more likely to go for this type of scam than women are. What evidence there is for this is unclear, but scammers don't tend to be wrong when it comes to profiling the right people for their ruse.

The email will usually have a subject line which expresses a romantic interest in you personally, along the lines of 'I saw your pictures and liked what I saw' or similar. The text of the email will briefly explain who the writer supposedly is. It will invite you to click on a link, which will apparently take you to a website where this person is on camera.

While this may genuinely be the case, at this point it's likely that a request for credit card or debit card details will be necessary for you to gain access to the site. They've got you on the hook, thinking a potential romantic interest might be behind that request. This is where the scam will really begin – even though the fee to access the site will be small and will likely result in you seeing someone on camera, they're not going to have the faintest idea who you are and you will probably be on a website that is accessed simultaneously by hundreds or thousands of other people. They never had any romantic interest in you – it was just a lure to get your card out of your wallet.

Essentially, you've just handed over your card details to a deeply unscrupulous company or group, who will then use and abuse them as soon as possible. You may see uninvited purchases on your card and direct debits set up in your name to companies you've never heard of. All this will need quick action via contact with your bank's fraud department and a potentially slightly embarrassing explanation as to how your bank

< 116 >

details were obtained in the first place – these kinds of sites often have quite literal names. It will also result in the inconvenience of needing a new card, but this all pales in comparison to the fact that your bank details have been compromised and are now in the hands of criminals.

THE TELLS

Out-of-the-blue approach.

The lure (an attractive offer to tempt you).

SEXTORTION

While we're on the subject of scams related to sex, this is one of the most desperately awful scams around at the moment. It has, sadly, resulted in several young men between the ages of sixteen and twenty committing suicide. Please, once you have digested this passage, get the information out to anyone you can in that demographic. It is also worth mentioning that this scam could also fit into the social media category, as it is just as likely to come in the form of an out-of-the-blue message from an attractive stranger on social media as it is in this email form.

You receive an email out of the blue that is deeply troubling and threatening in its tone. The emailer claims that because of some illicit websites you've been visiting, they have hacked your computer. You may read this and think, 'I don't visit illicit websites,' and this may well be true, but it is absurd to pretend that no one does. It is this category of website that the emailer will be referencing, and they will even go so far as to mention a few popular sites.

< 117 >

Using this angle of attack, the scammer will claim that in visiting those sites, they have managed to install malware on your computer or phone. Malware is a program designed with bad intentions; it is different from a traditional computer virus because it is usually used with some kind of specific intention beyond damaging a computer or phone, and it probably can't self-replicate and spread.

A good example, and perhaps the most frightening, is what the scammer will claim they have installed on your device through your visits to pornography sites. It is called a Remote Access Trojan, or RAT. A Trojan virus is like a Trojan horse – it is something installed on your computer by you or someone else which looks perfectly harmless, but within it contains extremely damaging computer code that allows a number of potentially scary events to occur. The RAT is the most worrying of these, because it gives whoever is controlling it the ability to use your device without your knowledge. They essentially become a second user, in the background, with access to all your files and all the same functions as you have yourself.

The scammer will state that using their hacked access to your device through the RAT, they have turned on your device's camera without your knowledge. They will claim that using that access, they have recorded video footage of you in your most intimate moments. Should you not be willing to comply with their requests, they plan to release the video to all your contacts, to which they also have access thanks to the RAT. Their closing sentences will explain that if you contact the police, they will release the video. If you try to wipe your computer or phone, they will know and release the video. Your only option, therefore, is to pay their ransom – they will then leave a cryptocurrency wallet address and demand payment within a certain time frame.

The most important consideration here is that it is first of all extremely, extremely unlikely that any scammer would have the

< 118 >

technical skills necessary to get a RAT installed on your device. Hackers with that level of skill do not tend to go after private individuals; they take on much bigger and more profitable targets like banks, or put their skills to good use (and make good income) by getting involved in cybersecurity, penetration testing (checking big corporations' websites for security vulnerability) and other similar professions.

As mentioned earlier, there is also a social media direct message version of this appalling scam, which takes a slightly different shape. It will actively target young males with a relationship status of single on their social media profile. The scammer will message out of the blue, appearing to be an attractive young woman of a similar age. They will likely claim a mutual friend, or set up the profile to seem to be from a similar area to their target. Their initial messages will express romantic interest in the target and start the process of flirtatious chat. This will lead to requests for photos of one another. As the relationship progresses, the scammer will share intimate photos of the woman (of course these are stolen from a real person) and encourage the man being targeted to do the same.

The moment the victim shares an intimate image, the tone of the conversation will immediately change. The scammer will reveal themselves and explain that unless the victim pays up immediately by a method of the scammer's choosing, they will release the intimate photo to their family and friends. Obviously, this will cause huge feelings of shame and embarrassment for anyone, and perhaps particularly for a teenager. In this situation it is very difficult to remain calm and consider what the genuine consequences would be even if the scammer did send out the images to family and friends, and if they can't pay up, the victim's shame and embarrassment has resulted in the appalling tragedies outlined above. Again, once you've digested this information, please pass it on to any younger men in your family.

< 119 >

THE TELLS

(Email version of the scam)

Out-of-the-blue approach.

Shame and blame (making you feel embarrassed or ashamed of your actions).

Unusual payment methods (gift cards, cryptocurrency, international or bank transfer).

Informational advantage abuse (claiming to know something you cannot verify).

(Social media version)

Out-of-the-blue approach.

The lure (an attractive offer to tempt you).

Shame and blame (making you feel embarrassed or ashamed of your actions).

Unusual payment methods (gift cards, cryptocurrency, international or bank transfer).

THE FAKE INVOICE SCAM

This email scam revolves around the use of panic-inducing, yet entirely fake, invoices to make you believe you have been scammed already. These will come from what appears to be a major online payment provider, not a bank whose security for this kind of transaction is harder to bypass

< 120 >

but a third-party company with whom you may have an account as an alternative means of paying online. For the purposes of explaining this scam without getting sued, we can call this payment provider 'StapletonPayments'.

Arriving in your inbox, the email from StapletonPayments will appear entirely legitimate, nicely designed with all the correct fonts and colours for the genuine payment provider's style. It will be a confirmation invoice for the purchase of a high-value item, listing your email address as the buyer – the scammer hoping that you use the same email to log in to any account you might have with StapletonPayments.

This will cause you deep concern, because it will seem to all intents and purposes that without your knowledge, someone has bought something worth a lot of money (most commonly electrical items) using your StapletonPayments account. Luckily, the scammer's email contains a number you can call if you don't recognize the transaction, to get through to StapletonPayments's customer service department. It suggests you need to call within twenty-four hours if you did not make the purchase.

This number is nothing to do with the genuine StapletonPayments; it's going to put you through to the scammers themselves, who will then perform an excellent impression of a genuine customer service representative of a tech company. They will ask you to read out the reference number of the invoice, how much it was for and which items. They will also need you to confirm your details, but again, this will be information gathering – apart from your phone number, at this point they'll know nothing about you because their email probably went to tens if not hundreds of thousands of people. They will then walk you through a version of one of the online shopping scams described in the phone call scams section of this book, most likely one which involves you either needing to move funds to a safe account (theirs) or to go through a convoluted process to receive a refund, which in fact ends up with them stealing your money instead.

< 121 >

THE TELLS

Out-of-the-blue approach.

Pressure, impression of urgency.

Unusual actions (moving around large amounts of money, sharing one-time passcodes).

Requests for excessive personal information.

THE OUTDATED BILLING INFORMATION SCAM

An email arrives in your inbox from what seems to be absolutely any company you pay a subscription fee to on a monthly basis, most likely by direct debit or similar. The email states that your billing information for the debit is no longer valid and needs to be updated.

These phishing emails will contain a link for you to update your information, as well as some threatening language suggesting that if the update isn't completed in a certain time frame, your account for whatever the subscription relates to will be deleted, or your credit rating affected or similar. If you follow the link, you'll be taken through to a clone website of the real organization, where you will be asked to enter new payment information. Should you do this, you'll be donating card details or account details to scammers. While this most likely won't cost you anything in the immediate sense, it will leave your banking wide open to more serious future scams and these scammers will likely use the information you've donated to set themselves up for something much more profitable, like impersonating your bank.

< 122 >

THE TELLS

Pressure, impression of urgency.

Requests for excessive personal information.

Dodgy URL (the web address is not the official website of the company it claims to be).

UNUSUAL ACTIVITY ON YOUR ACCOUNT (NOT BANKING)

This scam is another email intended to cause you immediate panic. It will relate to the account you use every day on your computer, phone or tablet, most likely an account with either Apple, Google or Microsoft.

Nowadays, most of us are signed in to an account with one of these three companies on a day-to-day basis, even though it's not necessarily something we notice too much. If you are on the internet regularly, you might well be signed in to a Google account to use their Chrome internet browser. If you have an iPhone, you're signed in to your Apple account, known as iCloud, to do anything. If you're an Android user, you're signed into a Google account to do anything. If you're using a Windows PC, it's likely you're signed in to a Microsoft account of some kind, maybe Outlook or similar. Either way, these accounts and cloud-based computing now form part of the background of all our lives, so an email stating that there has been unusual activity on an account that you are signed in to every single day is very alarming.

< 123 >

The email will request that if a sign in which occurred in a 'Far Off Country' wasn't you, then you should click on the link to verify yourself. If you click through, you'll be taken to a beautiful clone of a genuine website of one of the above companies. It will request that to verify yourself as the owner of the account, you need to sign in, and it will contain boxes to fill in your username and password.

The moment you do this, you will be giving your password and username to scammers. What can happen next is varied, but it is most likely that the scammers will immediately use this information to log in to your account from where they are. If you don't have 2FA set up (two-factor authentication, essentially meaning that when someone logs in to your account from a new or unrecognized device you will either receive a text to your phone or an email, or a request through an authentication app to tell you and ask if it is you before it is allowed), they will have access immediately. They will then begin altering contact details in the account. This will effectively lock you out of your own account. All the while, the scammers will raid it for everything they can get – personal details, payment details and your contact information. They will contact you shortly afterwards, telling you that you need to pay them to regain control of your account.

Should you find yourself in this situation, whatever you do, don't pay, because the scammers will only extort you for more money. Your best move here is to contact the company who control the account and explain that you've been hacked as soon as possible. If you're still logged in and there's the possibility to use the 'log out of all devices' option within the account's settings, do that, then attempt to use your two-factor authentication to log back in and reset your password.

< 124 >

THE TELLS

Pressure, impression of urgency.

Requests for excessive personal information.

Dodgy URL (the web address is not the official website of the company it claims to be).

THE COPYRIGHT STRIKE

A very similar approach to the above, but this email tends to be directed at the owners of businesses using social media to promote and sell their products. It comes in a few shapes, most commonly by email, but can also come from what might appear at first glance to be a customer service representative on social media.

The email version works like this: an email will arrive at the address you use for your business, claiming to be from the social media platform where your business's page exists. It will explain that your business's page faces closure or suspension due to a copyright claim from a big company with an interest in music, images or film. The email will provide you with a link to click on, claiming to take you to an appeal form. This link will even appear to take you to the correct website for the social media platform your page is registered with.

When you click through, sure enough you will see a message within the social media site that your business page uses. It will advise that you have a time limit to fill out the form, which requires you to click another link. This link will take you somewhere else entirely, but likely to a beautiful clone of the social media company's 'business help centre' or

< 125 >

similar. Here, you will be requested to fill out your business page's details and, crucially, to enter your password.

This will again pass your details to the scammers, who will then log in to your business account and change the contact details for any two-factor authentication you may have set up. You'll then face an experience similar to the above, being forced to pay to regain control as the scammers claim they will delete the page you may have spent years building up if you don't comply. Worse still for your reputation, the scammers will likely use your business page to try to defraud your customers while they have control. This may mean they send messages offering to sell items you have but doctoring payment details to go to them, for example. They might even begin posting banned content from your page to terrify you into paying, believing they will stop and you'll get control of your account again. But they won't stop – if you pay, they'll just keep extorting you for more, so your only option will be to go through the painful process of contacting the social media company to try to recover your hacked account.

THE TELLS

Out-of-the-blue approach.

Pressure, impression of urgency.

Requests for excessive personal information.

Dodgy URL (the web address is not the official website of the company it claims to be).

< 126 >

REQUEST FROM THE BOSS

This scam has been doing the rounds in a big way in 2024, and that tends to be a sign that it's very effective. The reasons why are pretty clear – it plays on the power dynamics of the workplace to get you to act quickly and without thinking too clearly about what's being asked.

You receive an email (this can be to a work or your personal address) that appears to come from the CEO of the company you work for. They are requesting your help with an urgent task. This can take two shapes – the most common being that the boss explains they are buying gift vouchers for you and your colleagues as an end-of-quarter bonus. Unfortunately, they have left their wallet at home or in the car, or have been mugged recently, or had a card blocked. Can you buy the vouchers and they will refund you asap?

This could be of a value of anything from the low hundreds to thousands in vouchers. Should you go for it – after all, this is your boss's boss's boss speaking – they will request that you send them the codes on the back of the vouchers, at which point, to the scammer posing as your boss's boss's boss, they're effectively cash – you won't be getting any of it back.

Version two sees the CEO send you an invoice and request your help in getting it paid immediately – in this version you will most likely be a human resources employee with access to payroll, or someone who works in the finance department of your company. Should you go through with it, the details on the invoice will be doctored and you will be paying scammers.

Here's the really clever part of the scam – the scammers may actually be emailing from your boss's boss's boss's actual email address, if they have managed to hack it. On top of that, when sending, they will have deleted it from the sent items folder in their email, and again from deleted items, so your boss's boss's boss will have no way of knowing it ever happened.

If they are really good at this, they will even set up a rule, which

< 127 >

is essentially a process by which the email server will treat any future messages from you. The rule will mean that your messages in response will go straight to your boss's boss's boss's archive folder instead of to their inbox, so the real CEO won't even see your replies. Only the scammers will know to check the archive and continue the conversation with you.

If the scammers haven't hacked their email, they'll likely use a close approximation of what their personal email could be. Either way, it's extremely difficult for you to work out that it isn't your boss's boss's boss.

The reason this scam works so well is the aforementioned power dynamic: are you really going to question the boss's boss's boss? The only advice here is to talk to your immediate manager and pass this one up the chain – no one is going to punish you for doing your due diligence, more likely they'll view you as a thorough employee.

THE TELLS

Pressure, impression of urgency.

Unusual payment methods (gift cards, cryptocurrency, international or bank transfer).

THE DOCUMENT SHARER

This is another work-related scam email, which will appear to come from a colleague sharing an online document with you. In the days of everything being saved on 'the cloud' (basically just meaning it's stored online instead of locally on your computer or phone itself), it's not

< 128 >

uncommon to receive a document in the course of your work day which is only accessible by clicking on a web address through a link.

The difference here is that the link will be carefully disguised but bogus. Should you click through, you'll taken to a login page for whatever organization runs your cloud-based document sharing and saving. This will be a clone, entirely fake and designed just to get you to enter your login information.

Should you go for it, much like the unusual activity scam above, you will find your account quickly hacked. This can be particularly dangerous in a corporate context, as the scammers will likely use their hacked access in the background to look for financial information they can abuse, invoices they can doctor and send, or valuable data like that of customers or other businesses.

THE TELLS

Dodgy URL (the web address is not the official website of the company it claims to be).

THE SOLICITOR SCAM

As far as all the scams in this book go, the solicitor scam might be the most potentially stressful. It uses the means by which we purchase and sell property in the UK against us, turning what is already a deeply stressful experience, probably one of the most stressful of our lives, into a deepening nightmare. Although this example is quite UK-specific, no doubt similar types of scam will exist elsewhere with minor tweaks to suit local property-buying systems.

When buying a home, there comes a point in the process where you

< 129 >

have to make what is almost certainly the single largest transaction you've made in your life – sending your deposit, or whatever amount it is you're paying towards the purchase of the property, to a solicitor. In the UK, all the paperwork and exchanging of money is handled by a solicitor (a property-focused lawyer) whose job it is to deal with the vendor's solicitor and facilitate the process of the purchase or sale. We put our trust in these solicitors to ensure that everything goes smoothly and that there will not be any interference in their communications with us. Unfortunately, scammers have cottoned on to the idea that if they are able to somehow gain access to a solicitor's emails, in the world of remote communications they may well be able to make some very large thefts indeed.

It works like this – you have been through the process of buying your home and are right at the point of the 'exchange' of contracts, one step away from getting the keys. To complete the exchange, you need to send your deposit or the total funds you're contributing across to the solicitor's account to be held until the moment of completion of the transaction. You have been told by your solicitor on the phone or by email that today is the day and to expect a message from them with details of where to send the money.

An email arrives from your solicitor's address, providing the information of the account to send monies to in the form of an invoice, bearing all the details you're expecting. You set up the transaction and send the money in its entirety. Later that day, you receive a second email from your solicitor asking you to send the money and providing the details. You explain that you have already sent it. The solicitor asks you to check the details of the transaction – how could you have sent it already when they have only just provided you with the details?

The solicitor's emails have been hacked by scammers. They have sent you a doctored invoice from your solicitor's actual address and in the process stolen your entire deposit. This not only leaves you tens or even hundreds of thousands of pounds out of pocket, it also threatens the

< 130 >

entire purchase of the property. Will you get the money back from your bank? Will you be able to buy the home you've been in negotiations for, probably for weeks, if not months?

It is just the beginning of the realization that you've been scammed, but the consequences to your life can be potentially absolutely hideous. The only way to protect yourself from it, which, knowing about this scam, I did when buying my home – is to call the solicitor directly once you have received the message and double-check the details with them in person on the phone. It's probably the biggest transaction you'll ever make, so no one will judge you for being as sure as you can possibly be.

THE TELLS

Dodgy documentation (fake invoices etc.).

THE 'REMEMBER THIS?!' SCAM

Very, very simple but very, very effective, this is an information-gathering exercise that relies on your intrigue to get you to comply. You receive an email that seems to come from a close contact, with the subject line 'Remember this?!' or similar. The message will likely be short and sweet, along the lines of 'Hi XX, I can't believe you did that! So much fun. Lots of love, YY.' It will also contain a link to click on, which will possibly have some photography-related words in the title to make you believe you're about to click through to some kind of photo storage website. What is most likely about to happen is your device is going to be riddled with malware the moment you click on the link, leaving you vulnerable to future scams, hacking and data theft.

< 131 >

When you click through there will be some other blocker to being able to see the supposedly shocking or funny image of you – like the need to create an account, for example. Again, this is just an attempt to get further information from you, because as you have hopefully worked out by now, it doesn't exist.

THE TELLS

Dodgy URL (the web address is not the official website of the company it claims to be).

Requests for excessive personal information.

THE NIGERIAN PRINCE (ADVANCED FEE FRAUD)

This scam is well spelled out in Chapter 2: The Scam Map of the World, but it now takes so many different shapes and forms, it's worth knowing them to be totally on top of the latest. The most common version of this advanced fee fraud, seen landing in email inboxes in the 2020s, is probably the 'distant relative' narrative. This is an email purporting to come from the executor of someone's will, and it will likely even have details of the law firm that this executor works for. The law firm itself could be legitimate, but the scammer sending the email will be using a fake employee name, which if you do some research about the law firm, won't be there.

They will explain in their message that a distant relative of yours has died in a far-off land and left you a substantial chunk of their enormous fortune. The job of the email is to make sure the funds

< 132 >

from the deceased's estate reach everyone they are supposed to. The money is unfortunately stuck in a complicated arbitration process until such time as you can provide the relevant documentation to receive it. To get your share, you will need to provide photo ID to the lawyer, proving who you are. You will also need to pay a fee to have the funds released to you. This works on two levels for the scammer, because with the prospect of a huge windfall coming your way, you not only pay them but give them your ID as well. This can then be used the next time they need to 'prove' who they are to their next unsuspecting victim. It's also worth noting that the scammer will probably want to be paid in some relatively obscure method like sending money by Western Union or, if they are slightly more professional, by international bank transfer to an actual account in the country they claim the death occurred in.

THE TELLS

Out-of-the-blue approach.

The lure (an attractive offer to tempt you).

Advance fee (a small upfront payment to secure a future benefit, e.g. money).

Requests for excessive personal information.

Unusual payment methods (gift cards, cryptocurrency, international or bank transfer).

< 133 >

5

Text Scams

Did this text message come out of the blue?

Assume it's a scam.

Does the text contain concerning information, time pressure or seem intended to panic you?

Legitimate organizations will never phrase their communications in a way that would cause you to panic. Take a breath and ask someone you trust their view on the message if possible.

Does it contain a link?

If the text contains a website to click through to, this is very likely to be risky, so follow the remaining steps first.

Does the content of the text read like a legitimate corporate communication?

Real texts from genuine companies will rarely if ever contain spelling mistakes or poor grammar and will likely be neutral in tone.

Thoroughly verify all the information in the text before engaging with it.

Call the organization concerned. Did they send this text? If there's a name or number for the sender, check it's the one used by that organization when sending texts. If the text contains a link, check the organization's official website using a search engine first, to see if it matches.

< 135 >

THE MISSED DELIVERY

If the 'Hi Mum' scam was arguably the Western world's most popular text scam in the past few years, if not ahead of it, this one has to be a close second. It relies on so many of us now having items delivered directly to our homes to spring us into action believing something has gone wrong. For a scammer, it's the perfect approach, combining ubiquity (almost everyone has items delivered with some regularity), the need for action and urgency, and the exchange of information.

You will receive a text that appears to come from a delivery service. It's very easy for scammers to spoof the title of the sender of messages these days, so whoever the text shows up as coming from on your smartphone, it doesn't matter – that information is not to be trusted. The text beneath will explain that unfortunately you have missed a delivery, and to have redelivery attempted there is a small fee. Usually this will be very small, in the region of £3.

To pay the fee, you'll see a link to click on, which will lead you through to a clone website representing the delivery firm. You'll need to enter your personal details, as well as some payment information like a long card number, expiry date and security code. If this was a legitimate request, it's far more likely you would only be asked for partial information like your postcode and some kind of reference for the delivery itself – by the same token, not many (if any) delivery companies currently charge fees to redeliver items. In giving this data over, you are not only giving your money to scammers but worse still, you are also setting yourself up for more serious scams down the road. It's very easy for a scammer to pose convincingly as your bank if they have a full card number and other card details.

< 136 >

THE TELLS

Dodgy URL (the web address is not the official
website of the company it claims to be).

Requests for excessive personal information.

THE PAYMENT ATTEMPT BANK SCAM

This is the 'fraudulent transactions on your account' approach you may remember from Chapter 3: Phone Call Scams, but re-versioned for text messages. The text will claim to be your bank's fraud department, reaching out as they are concerned about certain transactions made by your account – they may even list worrying amounts and purchases of items you have not made yourself.

There are two routes of attack for the scammer by text here – the most common is to leave a landline number for you to call to contact 'the fraud department' of your bank, but you will actually reach the scammer. If you go ahead with this, you'll then be guided through a phone call-based bank impersonation scam, as described in Chapter 3. The second (and less common) approach is to send a link for you to click on which will take you through to a clone website of your bank, where you will be requested to log in to your online banking to deal with the issue. In doing so, you will be giving the details for your online banking to the scammers – depending on your set-up for online banking, this may allow them to log in to it from their end and start transferring money out.

< 137 >

THE TELLS

Out-of-the-blue approach.

Pressure, impression of urgency.

Unusual actions (moving around large amounts
of money, sharing one-time passcodes).

THE TAX REBATE

In no way dissimilar to tax-related phone call scams, the beauty of the rebate scam from a scammer's perspective is the strength of their lure. As ever, the scammers move with the times, and during a cost-of-living crisis the notion of having overpaid tax to the extent that you are about to receive a lump sum back from the government is a very powerful one. For reasons of realism, this scam is most prevalent in February and March in the UK, when many people have just submitted their tax return, which is done at the end of January.

The text will arrive, likely appearing to come from the government's tax office, or spoofing a sender's name similar to theirs. In the UK this might be a close approximation of the real title, HMRC, like 'HMRCREBATE' or 'HMRCUK-TAX'; in the US it would be the IRS, so perhaps 'IRS-USA' or 'IRS-TAX', to give the scam the best chance of you believing it is genuine. Within the text itself will be a short explanation of the idea that you have overpaid on your tax return and are due a rebate. It will likely specify an amount in the low thousands to get your blood pumping.

The last step will be to try to get you to click on a link, which will take

< 138 >

you to a clone of the government's genuine online platform or portal for dealing with your taxes. Here, you will be asked to enter sensitive personal information to prove who you are, like your date of birth, address, name, unique taxpayer reference (UTR) and the account you would like the money paid into.

This is a very serious information-gathering exercise designed to extract high-level financial details from you using the lure of a substantial rebate. If you give this information over, you are likely to be on the receiving end of some very nasty future scams, either approaches out of the blue from bank or tax office impersonators, or attempts to set up payments in your name without your consent. It is also possible that using this information, the scammers might be able to commit other tax-related fraud against you, such as attempting to take over your tax affairs and claim any future rebates you are genuinely due, by posing as an accountancy firm. More on that later …

THE TELLS

Out-of-the-blue approach.

The lure (an attractive offer to tempt you).

Requests for excessive personal information.

Dodgy URL (the web address is not the official website of the company it claims to be).

< 139 >

THE JOB OPPORTUNITY

Yet another scam that plays on the financial insecurities affecting so many during difficult economic times globally, this scam almost always begins with an out-of-the-blue approach from a scammer claiming to represent a job agency.

The majority of these scams arrive by instant messaging applications (WhatsApp or Telegram, for example, which are encrypted, meaning the content of messages can't be seen by the authorities) rather than traditional SMS texts. Texts are too easily blocked as possible scams by the filters mobile operators have in place.

With so many people looking for new jobs, alternative sources of income and remote or flexible options to earn more money, the 'in' for the scammers is quite simple. The message will enquire as to whether you are interested in working from home on your own terms, for a pay package which seems very attractive (this will vary, but will always be at least £100 a day), and if so to respond yes.

Once you have responded, you'll be passed on to a second scammer who claims to work for the same agency. They may even have evidence of their supposed employment, sending you web links to look at for real companies and documentation to suggest they work for the agency concerned. Were you to call the agency yourself, you would quickly find out no such employee exists.

The second scammer will explain the work to you and ask if you are interested in beginning training. They tell you they will set you up with an account on what they claim is the platform designed by the employer. It will be a well-designed website, featuring known-brand logos and various different functioning, clickable areas to reassure you. They will explain that your pay will be commission-based, you will make as much money as the work you do. They will train you in 'the work', which is almost always an unbelievably menial task, such as

< 140 >

rating applications out of five stars or clicking on logos. The scammer's justification for this will be to explain that you are helping to drive customer engagement to the (entirely real) brands whose logos you see, or helping them with positive reviews, even though they have nothing to do with this at all.

This is, to some extent, a genuine type of work. There are companies all over the internet who will engage in what is known as 'reputation management', flooding new companies' sites with reviews from supposed customers, or helping to reverse the ailing online reputation of a certain brand with false positive experiences from customers posted on social media and sites which host supposedly genuine customer reviews.

What you are doing for these scammers, however, is totally bogus – it has no value. They have merely set up an entire online platform to make it appear that it does. As you are trained and click through logos or products or give reviews, you will see your 'account' being filled with 'commission', giving you the genuine impression that you are working for the company.

As part of the training, the scammer will almost certainly explain that to be paid, you will need a cryptocurrency wallet – they are a modern business and operate internationally, so paying in cryptocurrency is how they do things. This is not normal and should not be accepted as such, whatever they might say. They'll also likely drop into conversation that they have made 'a deposit' on your behalf, to get you up and running.

Once you have completed training, the scammer will add you to a group chat on your instant messaging platform, full of other employees extolling the virtues of this brilliant job. Your trainer will then suggest you do some work of your own whenever you're ready. On your first day of doing this, something will happen – as you click through logos or rate items on their platform, you'll receive a message telling you that you have a kind of 'super task' to do – they might call

< 141 >

it a 'multiplier task' or similar. It will suggest that by completing it, you will be able to earn three or four times more commission.

It's highly likely that you will go for this, tempted by the prospect of huge income. Should you do so, you will find that the account where your wages are filling up will suddenly drop into the red, maybe by as much as £1,000–£2,000. Confused, you will go back to your group of employees and trainer and ask them for help. The other employees in the group will tell you it's great news – just deposit some money to get the account back into the black, and you'll be earning three to four times your commission and make it all back and then some in no time.

Your trainer agrees and shows you how to do this – so you deposit £2,000. Sure enough, it works and suddenly your wages are filling up again. Your trainer even suggests that now is a good time to pay out from your account, so they help you organize it, showing you that it's easy to take funds out. You take out your wages from that day, £250. It appears in your cryptocurrency wallet as promised and you send it across to your bank account in pounds. It appears.

At this point, you are fully convinced. What scam would pay you money? You may have put in £2,000 of your own money, but earning £250 a day in commission, you'll have that back and then some in no time.

The next time you go back to work, another multiplier task or super task appears. It sends your account £5,000 into the red, but you know that you only need to deposit that money and do a few hours' work to get into the black again, and you'll be back in credit. So you deposit the money and go to work.

A few days later, your account is up to £6,000 in pay from all the commission you've been earning at this higher rate set up by the super task. When you come to withdraw your money, however, it fails. You try to contact your mentor, but their account is no longer visible on your phone. The group you were in with other employees no longer exists.

< 142 >

When you try to log back in to your account on the employer's platform, your account details do not work: you have just been scammed for the best part of £7,000.

This scam is complex and deeply psychologically manipulative, because in essence it works on us in the same way as gambling – do we put down some money with the prospect of winning big through our super task? It's tempting when you know that you might be paid three to four times the wages you would if you didn't do it.

The use of a support group also helps – we believe we are seeing others with experience telling us that this job is real and it works. That kind of supposed peer review is intoxicating. It was, however, also totally fake, the entire group populated by other scammers in the same office as your trainer, all ready to go with reassuring words for the victim, you.

The red flags with this one are quite complicated, beyond just psychological tells or actions. First of all, no employer should be taking you on without a contract, proper onboarding process, checking out your right to work and even an interview. Secondly, the pay is likely high – does it really reflect your experience of this kind of work? Is it unrealistic? While the scam has indeed paid you some amount of money in wages, what you have deposited has resulted in a net loss – does that feel like the behaviour you'd expect of a genuine company? All these points should be conversations you have with yourself when experiencing an approach like this, and it is always a good idea to run them past someone you trust if you're in this situation, whether that is a family member or friend, or even someone who will deal with this type of situation professionally, like a lawyer.

< 143 >

THE TELLS

Out-of-the-blue approach.

The lure (an attractive offer to tempt you – in this case, the super task leading to higher pay).

Unusual payment methods (gift cards, cryptocurrency, international or bank transfer).

Advance fee (a small upfront payment to secure a future benefit, e.g. money).

SIM SWAP SCAMS

This is a very tricksy scam that uses almost none of the usual psychological tells or strange actions we associate with most scams, and worst of all, it can have truly horrendous consequences. Advance warning: it is quite complicated. The basis of the scam is the ease with which it is possible to move your mobile number to another network.

This was originally made so due to well-intentioned plans to make it easier for customers to change network. A system was created, known as PAC codes (porting authorization codes), in which once requested, you would be sent a text containing a code that you could then pass on to your new network of choice. This would make the process of identifying you and your request seamless, and in theory make it possible to change network in a matter of minutes. As I've said, a well-intentioned plan designed to make it easy for customers in the UK to switch it up if they are unhappy with what is being offered on a certain network.

Before you are even aware that the scam is happening, it is likely that

< 144 >

the scammers will have acquired some of your personal information – and they're going to need it. This could have been via any of the methods of phishing described above, or through a data leak by a corporation, or even hacking. Their first step, again while you are totally unaware, will be to try to impersonate you to your mobile phone provider. In their attempts to impersonate you, they will persuade your provider that you want to change your number to a new SIM card within the same network. This is incredibly clever, because it means there is no need for you to receive a PAC code to be passed on to a new network. Because you're staying in the same place, the number can just be moved across without notifying you, provided the scammers can impersonate you convincingly. With your mobile number now in the control of scammers, registered to a new SIM card they have in their possession, they will begin work using it to defraud you. Given the way so much of our personal and financial security online is set up, this will not be difficult.

Immediately, the scammers will start using your mobile number to try to generate one-time passcodes for accounts to bypass the passwords on things like your email and online banking, even posing as you in calls to your bank. In this way they will attempt to gain access to your banking and other payment accounts you may hold online. In the meantime, your only option is to try to get in touch with your mobile provider and explain the situation – this can be a very difficult and messy scam to get out of, so if you do suddenly lose the ability to make calls or texts and don't know why, try to use another phone to contact your mobile provider immediately. If you are at home, you will still be able to use your home internet (Wi-Fi) to email your provider too.

The other best bit of advice here relates to two-factor authentication (2FA) – to avoid being a victim of SIM swapping, use authenticator apps instead of your mobile as backup when setting up 2FA where possible. This will mean that rather than being sent a text to reset your password or prove who you are, you'll be asked for a code generated

< 145 >

by the authenticator app on your phone. This will get you around the issue of reset codes being sent by text to a number that is no longer registered to your SIM card and thus goes to scammers instead. If you do sign up for authenticator apps, remember to remove your mobile as an option for two-factor authentication on any accounts you can use an authenticator for instead. If you don't, scammers will just use the backup of your mobile number and the authenticator will be useless.

THE TELLS

Out-of-the-blue approach (the initial total loss of mobile signal will come as a surprise).

< 146 >

6

Social Media and
the Online World

Did you receive a message out of the blue?

Assume it's a scam.

If you are buying something through social media or a website you haven't seen before, have you verified the seller?

Check the seller's profile or website before buying anything from them. If a profile, check they are a real person, with photos, friends and a history on social media that give you confidence they're real. If it's a website you've clicked through to from an ad, check the address matches that of the legitimate site using a search engine, and if it's a business you haven't heard of, check reviews in multiple locations online, not just from one source.

Can anyone else verify the seller/sender of the message?

Financial dealings through social media are always a risk – is there anyone in the group/on the page you're buying from who has also bought from/dealt with this person who you could ask for a vote of confidence in them?

Are you being offered the chance to invest money?

Financial advice obtained through social media is highly unlikely to be legitimate, however good it might sound.

< 147 >

Thoroughly verify all the information before engaging with it any further.
Spend time researching the social media profile of the person you are dealing with as above, as well as whatever they are offering/selling/suggesting. Do the same with any website. If in any doubt, do not go ahead. You will never regret doing your due diligence.

PURCHASE SCAMS (AND A QUICK GUIDE TO SPOTTING CLONE WEBSITES)

Buying all manner of things online has never been easier, with new, faster ways to pay being developed all the time. It works in our favour as consumers by making all our shopping desires only a few taps away, and it works for the companies selling items by removing blockages to selling their wares – but it also works in favour of scammers, for whom taking your money with a fake website, or an item which doesn't exist, has also never been easier. Purchase scams are many and they vary massively, but the broad brushstrokes and the tells that will help you stay on top of them are common enough.

The most common type of purchase scam you might encounter in the online world is probably the clone website. This will likely originate with an advert you encounter, which could be on social media or elsewhere online. The advert will appear to link you to the website of a company you might recognize. When you click through, the clone website will look pretty much like the real thing. The item you are looking for from the advert will seem to be available to purchase.

If you fill in your payment and delivery details and pay, you will be charged, but you will never receive anything in return. These clone websites are not just good earners for scammers, they are also exercises in phishing – obtaining excellent, high-level personal and financial information from you at the same time as defrauding you.

< 148 >

Thankfully, spotting a clone is very easy when you know how. All clone websites will have a web address that is not the real address of the company they claim to be. So, immediately when clicking through from an ad, if you're expecting to be at the web address of my imaginary big-time online shopping site Stapleton's Emporium, head over to your search engine first and search for it to check what the official website is. You could even progress the transaction from here rather than going back to the link on social media.

Most likely it will be some iteration of the company's name, followed by '.com' or '.co.uk'. For example: www.stapletonsemporium. co.uk. If the address you find yourself at doesn't match the real one from the search engine, it's a clone. Check carefully – scammers love using tiny adjustments or common misspellings to trick you. In the case of my imaginary shop, they could buy up the web address www. stapletonemporium.co.uk, which is only one letter away from the real (imaginary) thing.

There are also almost always visual clues you can use to work out if the site you have ended up on is not legitimate. The first one is 'dead' links. When scammers design clone websites, it's highly unlikely they will go to the trouble of making an entire website with multiple different pages you can access, terms and conditions, contact us, all the bits and bobs you would usually expect to see. It's just too much work. As such, they tend only to design the parts of their scam site that will actually take your money off you. If you're suspicious, check the links around the site by clicking or tapping on them, and you may find they don't actually work or go anywhere at all, despite appearing to be real. This is a sure-fire sign the site is a clone – so click around. Can you access the company's Ts and Cs? Are you able to navigate to different parts of the shop where other products are available? Last but not least on the visual clues front is resolution. What I mean by that is the visual quality of the site itself. Almost every legitimate site you've ever been to will be beautifully put

< 149 >

together, with pin-sharp design and seamless colours and lines. A clone site might not be quite so perfect because it's been lifted from the original, and in moving it across to the scam site some of the beauty of the design may have been lost. Check the edges of the page – is there any distortion or pixelation? Can you see any blurred or rough edges?

One other indicator that has been helpful in the past is spelling and grammar, though with the rise of AI usage in designing these things it might become less so. Does the site have any obvious typing errors or sentences which don't land in English due to the scammers using automatic translation software? This could also be a good indicator that you've found yourself a clone.

Finally, price. Is the site you're looking at offering you the product you want at a price point far below its competitors? This is a *very* strong indicator that you're dealing with a scam site. How is this business able to price the product so much more competitively than anyone else? Be very careful if this is the case – it's highly likely to be a scam.

SPOTTING CLONE WEBSITES

Web address doesn't match official website.

Visual clues (e.g. dead links, poor resolution).

Incorrect spelling and grammar.

< 150 >

With all this in mind, you should be very safe from your most common purchase scam – however, there are less common varieties that can still trip you up. For example, scammers don't only use recognizable company names to scam you – they may set up sites offering desirable or known products, creating online shopping companies to sell them that look legitimate but which you've probably never heard of. That's not to be unfair on new businesses trying to break into the online sales market but just to offer a word of caution when it comes to sites you've never seen before.

The most important method you can be sure of here in terms of assessing whether or not they might be a purchase scam is again price comparison. If they're noticeably cheaper than any of their competitors offering the same thing, it's highly likely they may be about to scam you. You should also check that the site has a proper terms and conditions page, which should ideally have a registered company name behind it (a limited company if they're in the UK; there is no centralized database of companies in the US, but you can check sites like the Better Business Bureau for information).

If you really want to vet them thoroughly – if you're buying a slightly higher value item, for example – there's no harm in checking their supposed contact details, seeing if you can give them a call or look at their address on Google. You can also go to your search engine and search the site's name. Does the information all check out and match details for the business you can find elsewhere on the internet? Are there satisfied customers reviewing them well online, not just on their own site (which is very easy to fake) but on trusted, independent review sites? Or is there very little information about them out there? If the latter is true, pause before giving them a large amount of money, and it's always worth getting a second opinion from a trusted relative or friend too.

< 151 >

THE TELLS

Dodgy URL (the web address is not the official website of the company it claims to be).

Excessively cheap in comparison to other options.

Murky business details.

THE DUPLICATED POST SCAM (AND WHY FACEBOOK MARKETPLACE IS A SCAMMER'S PARADISE)

It is very difficult, when buying items online, to be absolutely sure that they actually exist. This is especially true of Facebook Marketplace, where an investigation by TSB in 2024 found that as many as a third of all items listed for sale could be scams.

Facebook Marketplace was never intended as anything more than an age of information version of the classified ads in the back of a newspaper. For that reason, it has become the frontier of the purchase scam world, where the consumer (either as buyer or seller) is responsible for protecting themselves against scams. Meta, Facebook's parent company, sees Marketplace as simply a 'meet up and collection' service, helping you to find people who want what you have to sell, or vendors with the product you're looking for. Meta's right of reply mentions the company's 'important role in tackling the industry-wide issue of online purchase scams' but notes that it does not 'facilitate payments or shipping'. The site is simply not designed with any in-built protection for the transaction – it all happens in any way you

< 152 >

want (cash, bank transfer, by other online payment apps), all out of Meta's sight and control.

Unfortunately that means that if the item you paid for doesn't actually exist or if your buyer scams you, Meta have no responsibility to refund you, and you have very little protection other than what your bank or whatever payment method you used might offer themselves. Given that is the case, being wide awake to the potential scams that are in regular use on a platform like Facebook Marketplace is essential, if you insist on using it.

The duplicated post – or 'item does not exist' – scam is incredibly easy for scammers to pull off on a platform like Marketplace. All you need to start posting items for sale there is a Facebook profile, and there is absolutely no need at all to prove who you are, where you are or to hand over any sort of identifying details to set one up. That being as it is, making an entirely fake profile is very easy and makes you very hard to track down. On top of that, as we go through the next segment you'll see that social media account hacking is extremely common and means scammers can use stolen, once-genuine accounts to run scams, making it even harder to work out who might be a real person, genuinely selling something, and who isn't.

On top of it being easy to start selling with either a fake or stolen profile on Marketplace, it's also exceptionally easy to sell a high-value item that simply doesn't exist or which you haven't got the right to sell. For example, what's to stop a scammer going onto a second-hand car sales website, finding a desirable vehicle for £15,000, saving all the photos and videos of it and copying the description, editing a few words to make sure it isn't a perfect match and then reposting it as for sale on Facebook Marketplace for £7,500? The answer is nothing.

You may question how this leads to someone being defrauded, given that the scammer can't let a possible buyer come and test-drive the vehicle, nor can they show evidence that they actually own it. The simple

< 153 >

answer is usually this: they will offer some excuse as to why it can't be seen temporarily (they're out of the country, the car is stored hundreds of miles away elsewhere) but if the buyer wants to secure it, if they're willing to place a deposit of 10 per cent then they can come for a test-drive when the seller is back home, or they can have it couriered to the buyer's house on a trailer.

The scammers selling high-value items like this on Marketplace will also almost always have official-looking invoices ready to go to reassure you; they may even talk to potential buyers on the phone several times in the process of the scam. Thoroughly check anything sent to you – does it have a company name attached? Research it. Research the number they are calling from. If none of it leads anywhere, it's highly likely it's just smoke and mirrors to cover a scam. If you pay a penny, the profile selling the car, the listing where it was for sale and your money will be gone, never to be seen again. It's that easy.

Apply this same logic to countless other high-value items on Marketplace – property rentals, electronics, trailers, white goods. Protecting yourself against it is very, very difficult, but the best rule of thumb is this: do not pay money for any item on Marketplace that you have not first seen in person.

My overall rule for the site, which goes beyond and above that, is do not deal in anything over a value you are willing to lose in its entirety. If you're willing to lose £100, then feel free to buy and sell up to that value. Everything else, buyer and seller beware. More on the selling scams relating to sites like Marketplace in Chapter 8: In-person Scams.

< 154 >

THE TELLS

Dodgy documentation (fake invoices etc.).

Fake profile (no posting history/photos/friends from area).

Excuses, excuses (you can't see the item
you're buying, for some reason).

SOCIAL MEDIA ACCOUNT HACK AND RANSOM

Is this the scam I receive more messages about from members of the public who have been a victim than any other? Quite possibly. If not, it's a close competitor. If you're not a social media user, it probably sounds faintly ridiculous, but the context of how most people use social media is really important.

Our social media profiles, particularly the likes of Facebook and Instagram, have become not just digitized representations of our identities (and often heavily PR'd ones!) but also our personal collections of treasured memories, a contacts book and a means by which we can feel close to distant relatives and long-lost friends. It's even sometimes how we grieve and remember those we have lost. Social media has become an all-encompassing tool by which we live and document our lives. That gives our profiles a huge intrinsic value on an emotional level for the vast majority of people who have personal accounts which they use regularly. Beyond that, there are now businesses for whom years of work, a customer base and positive reputation are all also held within the computer code that makes up a business profile on social media. This is what makes these profiles

< 155 >

an extremely attractive prospect for scammers. Anything that has this kind of emotional worth, scammers know they can use against us.

For the above reasons, the trade in hacked or leaked email and password combinations is booming on the dark web. The countless leaks of our data from corporations we have trusted with them, hacks by those with ill intent and our own carelessness in failing to observe good password security have made stealing social media accounts not just easy but extremely profitable for scammers.

You can use a brilliantly useful website like Have I Been Pwned (www. haveibeenpwned.com, 'pwned' is internet slang for hacked) to check your emails and phone numbers for how many times they have been breached in a data leak or hack. It's not a case of if, rather how many? One of my email addresses has been compromised on thirteen separate occasions. This doesn't need to be as alarming as it sounds, provided you check the dates of the hacks or leaks shown and make sure that you're not using any passwords from before they happened in combination with the compromised emails or phone numbers. It's most likely due to leaks and hacks such as this that the vast majority of social media account hackings occur: an email and password combo found for sale on the dark web, likely as part of a data set of thousands of others, which scammers then start to test against major social platforms. If you don't have two-factor authentication set up and the combo of email and password the scammers have bought works, they can successfully log in to your profile.

What comes next may vary, but the initial step the scammers will take is to change all the contact details on your account, ensuring any future correspondence related to it or their sudden login from a new location won't come back to you. Before doing that, they'll make a note of the details you had there already for a ransom note. Coming your way shortly, this will be an email or a text explaining what's happened and laying out the scammer's terms. Pay up, or they will delete your beloved account.

< 156 >

The payment request will almost certainly be for cryptocurrency and the amount based upon the perceived value of your account – if you are a successful business or an influencer with 100,000 followers on social media, a huge base of established clients or fans, or items for sale, you could be ransomed for thousands. An individual with a few hundred friends and a decade's worth of memories stored on their profile might only be asked for £500.

> Crucially, it's worth remembering that if you pay, you are unlikely to get access back – the scammers will just keep going until they think they've extorted you for all you're worth and never return the account.

In some serious cases, the worst that social media account hackers have done to try to extort money is to threaten the account holder with having their profile permanently deleted if they do not comply with payment requests. Worst-case scenario, they will post appalling (and illegal) content from your profile, such as child pornography or images of death. This will inevitably lead to your account being permanently suspended or deleted by the platform controlling it.

The only ways you can defend yourself against social media account ransom are by practising good password security (more than ten figures and letters, some capitalized and at least one special character, like an exclamation mark), regularly checking that the passwords used are not subject to data leaks using the method described above and of course setting up two-factor authentication on any account you care about.

THE TELLS

Pressure, impression of urgency.

Unusual payment methods (gift cards, cryptocurrency, international or bank transfer).

Advance fee (a small upfront payment to secure a future benefit, e.g. access to your account).

THE INVESTMENT GROUP SCAM

This social media scam is a good one to think about if you are invited to take part in any group chat with strangers online. The techniques used by scammers within this can be applied to numerous other scams in this book and often are, with particular reference to job scams and other investment scams.

This will always begin with a message out of the blue from an individual or business profile offering their services to help with an investment opportunity. If you are already in existing investment communities on social media, they will likely use this as their 'in', approaching with something along the lines of the following: 'I've seen you are in the group about Investing in XYZ, but I don't think it's that good. I've been using this one instead, join me.'

They will suggest an alternative page or group to join on social media. It may on the face of it appear to be fairly legitimate, perhaps even relating to a real investment business with a public-facing website, fancy headquarters and staff listed on the site. The social media version, however, will be a clone of the real business and absolutely nothing

< 158 >

to do with it, despite appearances. The scammers running the group or page will ensure that it is populated with fake profiles extolling the virtues of investing with the group, regularly sending messages citing their successes, with faked-up evidence of their earnings.

All this is a confidence trick designed to buy your trust. It is likely no more than a string of entirely fake social media profiles or bots under the control of one or two scammers. Don't be fooled – even if there are seemingly tens or even hundreds of people posting positively on the group about their experiences, this is all easily faked.

To part you with your money, you'll be coached via direct messages from a 'mentor' in the group on how to invest. This will almost inevitably involve setting up a cryptocurrency wallet. The mentor will also probably take you off the social media platform to do this (to avoid discovery and oversight) and into an encrypted messaging platform like WhatsApp, which should keep their activities away from the watchful eyes of the authorities. Once you've invested, you'll be sent evidence of your returns, most likely via the group. You will genuinely receive income too, but it's just a ruse designed to get you to invest more. Once the scammers feel that they have all they're going to get out of you, they'll simply kick you out of the group and page, and move on. You'll be blocked by all the profiles you thought were your investing colleagues. It will be as if it never existed, and they will move on to their next victim, creating the same theatre of investment fakery for them.

< 159 >

THE TELLS

Out-of-the-blue approach.

The lure (an attractive offer to tempt you).

Unusual payment methods (gift cards, cryptocurrency, international or bank transfer).

Fake profile(s) (no posting history/photos/friends from area).

MAN IN THE MIDDLE ATTACK (MITM)

This could just as well have fitted into Chapter 8: In-person Scams, but even though it does indeed take place when you are out in public, it is reliant on an internet connection. It is also hard to categorize in terms of 'tells', as there aren't really any conventional scam tells to it.

A 'Man in the Middle' (MitM) attack is a scam that, unlike most other scams which claim to involve it, actually does involve genuine hacking of your device. Imagine that you are at a train station – we'll call it Staple Street. Imaginary Staple Street station has free Wi-Fi, which means you can connect free of charge and without a password, and get online without the need to use your mobile data.

When you open your phone to look at the available Wi-Fi connections, you see one with full signal high up the list, which is called Staple_Street_FreeWiFi, so you connect to it. Unfortunately for you, this Wi-Fi is an MitM. It is not the free Wi-Fi provided by the station, which is actually called StapleStreetWifi. Signs around the station say as much, but you haven't spotted them.

< 160 >

Hackers, set up nearby, have set up a fake version of the station's Wi-Fi to enable them to access people's devices. Should you access it by mistake, you will be giving them access to your phone or computer, or whatever device you've connected to it. The nature of free Wi-Fi like this is deeply insecure – any connection that doesn't at least have a password is open to abuse by those who know how.

The MitM can be cleverly designed so that once you are connected to it, even though it's free it will ask you to set up an account with a username and password. This will require your email and a password, for which you'll most likely give one you commonly use. That will result in the hackers who set up the connection taking possession of that information. They can then use it to try to hack your social media accounts, your email etc. Depending on their level of skill, they may even be able to use their MitM to access your device itself. This could be through disguised requests for access, appearing as pop-up windows asking security questions or similar.

The beauty of the MitM is that it is very easy not to become a victim: just don't connect to free, passwordless Wi-Fi unless you are using a VPN on your device. With most VPNs, your connection is always encrypted, so your data will be safe even if you accidentally connect to the internet using an MitM connection.

THE TELLS

Free product (in this case, Wi-Fi).

< 161 >

ARTIFICIAL INTELLIGENCE SCAMS

Artificial Intelligence (AI) is poised to significantly transform the world of scams and fraud, both by enabling more sophisticated scams and by enhancing the tools available to prevent and detect fraudulent activities. The dual impact of AI – its potential both to empower scammers and protect against them – will shape the future landscape of cybercrime and security.

AI's capabilities in data processing, pattern recognition and natural language generation are already being exploited by cybercriminals to create more convincing and widespread scams. One of the most concerning developments is the use of AI to generate highly personalized phishing attacks.

Unlike traditional phishing attempts, which are often generic and easily recognizable, AI-driven phishing campaigns can analyse vast amounts of data – such as social media activity, public records and hacked information – to craft messages specifically tailored to individual targets. This makes it much harder for potential victims to distinguish these scams from legitimate communications. Moreover, AI can automate the process of identifying potential targets and launching scams at scale. For example, AI bots can be deployed to trawl through social media platforms, forums and other online spaces to identify vulnerable individuals or businesses. These bots can then generate and send thousands of personalized scam emails or messages within minutes, vastly increasing the reach and efficiency of fraudsters.

Another alarming application of AI is in the creation of deepfakes – highly realistic but fake videos or audio recordings. Scammers can use deepfakes to impersonate CEOs, celebrities or even close relatives, convincing victims to transfer money or reveal sensitive information. The realistic nature of deepfakes makes them particularly dangerous, as they can easily bypass traditional verification methods, such as phone calls or video chats.

< 162 >

While AI introduces new threats, it also offers powerful tools to combat scams and fraud. Financial institutions, cybersecurity firms and law enforcement agencies are increasingly leveraging AI to detect and prevent fraudulent activities. One of the key strengths of AI in this domain is its ability to analyse large data sets and identify patterns that would be impossible for humans to detect manually. For example, AI-driven fraud detection systems can monitor millions of transactions in real time, identifying unusual patterns or behaviours that may indicate fraudulent activity. These systems use machine-learning algorithms to study previous incidents of fraud, continually improving their accuracy and reducing false positives. This enables financial institutions to block or flag suspicious transactions almost instantaneously, preventing significant losses.

AI is also being used to enhance identity verification processes. Traditional methods of verifying identity, such as passwords or security questions, are increasingly vulnerable to being hacked or stolen. AI-based systems, however, can incorporate biometric data – such as facial recognition, voice analysis or even behavioural biometrics (e.g. typing patterns) – to create more secure and reliable forms of authentication. These methods are much harder to replicate or spoof, providing a stronger defence against identity theft and unauthorized access. Furthermore, AI can assist in tracking down and prosecuting fraudsters. By analysing patterns of online behaviour, AI can help law enforcement agencies identify networks of criminals and predict where future scams may emerge. This proactive approach not only helps in catching perpetrators but also in preventing scams before they can cause harm.

If you want to get a sense of just how good AI has got at impersonating us and our behaviour, what better example than the last 500 words? All of that was written by ChatGPT, using the prompt, 'Please explain in 500 words how AI is going to change the world of scams and fraud'.

< 163 >

Scary, right? As the AI already explained, it's a case of pros and cons, but the troubling bit is that, for the moment, we don't even have a handle on where it will all end. The possibilities of AI are expanding every day and the more intelligence it gains, by which we mean the more it learns, the more capable it will become.

Advice on how to avoid getting caught in any of the myriad AI-using scams out there is hard to come by, given the nascent stage of this field that we're in, but there are a few early ideas that should help protect us all.

When it comes to a phone call from a family member wanting to talk about money, it will unfortunately be possible for AI voice generators to create a very passable version of your nearest and dearest, provided there are lots of recordings available of that person for the AI to digest. If you like posting lots of videos of yourself online, it's a real danger. The more information there is about you available for a scammer to feed to an AI, the easier it will be for the AI to perfectly recreate you. Best practice here is to set up code questions or codewords to use with family members when discussing money. That might mean, for example, asking them immediately where you were when you met your partner, or what the name of your earliest family pet was. Alternatively, it can just be a pre-agreed phrase or word that you don't record anywhere online and which you all know to use when you're discussing sensitive financial information.

This isn't over-egging the pudding. It's essential to get ahead because AI scams will start to happen, and they already have – with a finance worker paying out $25 million after a video call with their employer's chief financial officer. The only problem? They were talking to an AI 'deepfake' of the CFO and paid that money to scammers.

< 164 >

THE KIDNAP SCAM

This is the perfect scam to follow a segment on AI, as it simply wouldn't work without the invention of AI voice generators. These are pieces of software that allow the user to enter recordings of a person's voice, which the AI will learn from. Once enough recordings have been submitted, the user will either be able to speak and have their voice sound exactly like that of the person whose recordings they used, or type in words and sentences that the AI will speak as the individual.

In the age of countless videos of ourselves being shared every day, this is not good. It means that if you have children with extensive online profiles, their voices can easily be faked. All a scammer will need to do is work out who your children are (if you have linked profiles on social media, this is very easy) and then find a sufficient number of your child's videos to be able to feed audio into a voice generator.

What follows is that you receive a phone call from someone who sounds exactly like your child. They explain that they are in serious trouble: they have been kidnapped and the group holding them are requesting £10,000 for their immediate release. Before you are able to start asking any questions a second voice takes over, explaining that what your child said is true, and if you want to see them again, you need to listen to their terms. They will explain how to pay and give you a short time period in which to do so, making clear that if you speak to the police, your child will be killed. Failure will also lead to your child's death.

At this point it is likely the call will end, to give you the chance to pay the money immediately. Should you fail to do so, the scammers will call again and allow the AI version of your child another chance to persuade you to make payment. The best course of action in this scenario is to try to contact your child directly to verify what the scammer is saying yourself, but placed in an irrational state by being given such

< 165 >

unbelievably distressing information, thinking of this kind of action is far easier said than it would be done.

The entire scam relies on the speed of your actions to get your money – the scammers will most likely request it to be sent by bank transfer or withdrawn as cash and left in a specific location within a very short time frame.

THE TELLS

Pressure, impression of urgency.

Isolating from sources of trust (in this case, the police).

< 166 >

DEEPFAKES AND HOW TO SPOT THEM

The first sentence of this segment can only deal with one thing: what on earth is a deepfake? Briefly mentioned previously, it is what happens when you combine AI with what is known as 'special effects' in the movie business. This allows anyone with access to video editing tools that combine these two things to create video that looks entirely genuine, but is not. Real-life examples from the recent past would be what appeared to be a video of Martin Lewis, aka MoneySavingExpert, extolling the virtues of investing in a new cryptocurrency, or Elon Musk doing the same. Both were entirely faked. These examples unfortunately led to investment scams similar to those described earlier in the book.

Deepfake videos are, as the name would suggest, entirely fake, but on the face of it they appear real, which is to say they appear to show the person speaking the words in their real voice. The easy definition is any image or recording that has been digitally altered to make that person say something or do something they never actually said or did.

For those who have never heard of a deepfake or don't know how to spot one, they can be extremely dangerous. Their uses also reach beyond the world of scams; they can quickly and powerfully spread misinformation, sow political division and help grease the wheels of a public shaming. Knowing how to tell the real from the fake is going to become an essential skill in the coming years, not just when it comes to keeping your money where it belongs.

< 167 >

The methods available for spotting a deepfake, whether a video, an image or an audio recording, are easy to learn, though some require effort and research on your part. Starting at the easier end of the spectrum, video, the most important thing to do is to look at the face. However good the special effects or AI might be, the face (as of early 2025, though this will get harder to spot as technology progresses) usually contains giveaways that are easy enough to spot.

The skin of the face may appear too smooth, or too wrinkly, the mouth shapes being made may not match the real mouth shapes needed to form the words you are hearing. Do the shadows and lines on the face make sense? Deepfakes struggle with the physics of a scene, so these might be odd or look slightly uncanny. Observe the individual's blinking closely – do they blink too much, or too little? All these are indicators that you are looking at a deepfake.

There are behavioural and practical clues you can find too – does this person seem to be behaving in line with their character? For example, have you ever seen Martin Lewis excitedly telling you about a specific investment opportunity before? The answer is no, because he only gives general advice around finances, not specific investments, ever. The practical clues you can look for yourself include checking if the official channels used by the individual you're seeing contain the same information. Is Elon Musk's official social media account promoting the same product you are seeing in the video? Any famous face with a product to sell will always do so via their official channels, not just in videos circulated on the internet generally.

Audio recordings, due to the lack of anything to observe closely, can be much harder to decipher as deepfakes. The tone of the

< 168 >

voice could be a good indicator — AI-generated voices are often considerably flatter and less sing-songy than the real rhythm and pitch of a genuine voice. Listen carefully: if the voice you are hearing is particularly monotone and lacking in those peaks and troughs, it is highly likely a deepfake. Background noise can also be an indicator — is there any? Is there too much, so it sounds uncanny or artificially laid on? Is there none at all?

You can also look at sources — *where* are you seeing this video or hearing this audio? *What* is the source? Does the source represent a trustworthy organization that has a long history of fact checking or verifying content? If the answer is no, take pause before believing what you hear. Can you find the clip's context elsewhere online? For example, if you are hearing an excerpt of what appears to be a politician caught off-mic saying something inflammatory, is there a longer recording of it available anywhere to give context? If not, why not? In the age of information, it is extremely unlikely that a single, short clip would exist without any wider context or association with a particular event or date.

Lastly, behavioural signs are again important. Is the person you are hearing behaving in line with that you know of their public personality? Are they saying something incredibly inflammatory or controversial? Have they stated that opinion publicly elsewhere, or is this single source the only evidence of it you can find?

Deepfake images are, thankfully, rather easier to spot, at least for now. Part of the reason behind that is AI image generation struggles a lot with aspects of detail. If you see an image online that appears to show something controversial, or shows a celebrity promoting a product or service, the devil is in the digits.

< 169 >

Seriously – look at the hands, fingers, and if they're visible, toes. What you will likely see is a bit of a mess: fingers that overlap or go places they physically can't, excessive wrinkling or total flatness of skin tone. Again, if there is any text in the image or on the person's body, study it closely. It will most likely be misspelled, confused or even complete gibberish.

The most important thing, however, is to look at the image as a whole. We tend to observe most things online with what you can call 'soft eyes', allowing visual content to wash over us without closely observing it. Instead, observe with extreme attention any image that is clearly geared to make you feel a certain way or take a certain action.

This is harder to put a specific meaning on but observe the image in its entirety: does it seem slightly animated, with softer lines and less depth than a real photo? Does it have a slightly uncanny or cartoonish appearance? Track the edges – is all the detail correct or are there missing or broken elements? All this will help you stay on top of this worrying and increasingly common type of scam. It is also essential in preparing you for what comes next.

THE TELLS

Altered or manipulated footage/audio/image.

< 170 >

SYMPATHY SCAMS, AKA 'GRANNY TRAPS'

This scam is unique in this book in that it doesn't (initially at least) actually involve the loss of any money. It will seem entirely harmless, in fact, and for most people who go for it, it will be. Among them, however, will be an unfortunate few for whom it's the beginning of a very ugly scam indeed.

Sympathy scams, which are cruelly known online as 'granny traps', are set-ups created by scammers on social media to make it easier for them to find suitable victims. They abuse the way in which social media works in order to ensure maximum exposure. If you imagine a long-line fishing vessel that drags a huge net across the ocean, catching whatever it may (including all manner of fishes it doesn't want) but only keeping the specific fish it's looking for, that is the methodology behind a 'granny trap'.

They work like this: scammers use an AI image generator to create an image they know will create feelings of empathy and positivity among their target audience. A good example of this might be a young child, seemingly from a third-world country, who has miraculously created a beautiful piece of art from recycled plastic bottles. Another would be an ageing soldier who has lost both their legs and has artificial limbs, in full uniform, celebrating their birthday with a cake. Both images are entirely fake, created by the scammers by entering a prompt phrase into an AI image generator: 'Create an image of an elderly soldier with no legs who is celebrating their birthday with a cake in their uniform.'

With the images in their possession, the scammers then post them on social media. They will post on popular pages their target audience enjoy, which may celebrate times past, request posts of inspiring images or other similar themes. Alongside the image of the child who has created the amazing art from rubbish, the scammer will post something along the lines of: 'Some art I created from plastic bottles with my own hands.

< 171 >

A like or a comment will cost you nothing. Why do my pictures never trend?' For the soldier it might be: 'Celebrating my ninetieth birthday today, give me a wish to thank me for my service.' The scammers' sole intention here is to generate a swell of likes and comments on their photo from anyone who sees it. They appeal to the humanity of those who see it with the caption, and the well-intentioned users of the social media site will like and comment in droves. The scammers will likely also use bot accounts (profiles that seem real but are robots controlled by the scammers to do specific tasks) to increase the number of comments and likes artificially.

Why? Because this is how social media works – the more comments and likes a single post gets, the more the social media platform will push that post into the feed or homepage of other people who have not seen it. This is how posts 'go viral'.

Now, why would a scammer want their post going viral? Because the more *real* people that comment and like the photo, the more the scammer is likely to find the specific person they are looking for to begin their scam. Best of all from the scammers' point of view, these victims are coming to them. They even get to see the potential victim's profile photo, if they have one, allowing them to weigh up who is best to go for.

Once their post has thousands of likes and comments, the scammers will go to work on those they think are the perfect victims for their scams. This will begin with seemingly innocent approaches in the comments, replying to a post from a potential victim. In the example of the child who has made the art, the victim may have replied to the post with something like: 'What a talented young man! Impressive work!' Seeing that this person cannot tell the image is AI is enough for the scammer to reply, using a fake account specifically tailored to what they think that individual would like: 'So beautiful! May I ask if we can be friends. You seem nice.' That will then see the

< 172 >

beginning of a romance scam. The scammer has used their original post to entice victims, vet them, research their social media profiles and create a perfect 'romantic partner'. All that from one simple AI image generator prompt.

Protecting yourself from this kind of trap is very easy – just don't engage with posts on social media unless you are certain they are not AI-generated or if they're clearly trying desperately to get you to engage with them. If you apply the rules above to work out if the image is AI and it proves to be, do not comment on it, do not like it. Even liking it alone is making others more likely to go for the trap themselves, as it will make the post more prominent.

THE TELLS

Out-of-the-blue approach (strangers wanting to be friends in the comments of the post or by direct message to your inbox).

Altered or manipulated footage/audio/image.

Bot account interaction.

BOTS, FAKE FOLLOWERS AND INFLUENCE

The importance of this section is not to be underestimated. This is not a traditional scam in the most basic sense, but much like the sympathy scam it is rather a tool scammers can use to help them in several significant ways.

Firstly, a quick definition of what a bot account actually is and does would be helpful.

< 173 >

A bot, in the online world, is an account that on the face of it appears real but is in fact automated and controlled by someone. What this means is that the bot account can be made to automatically perform specific actions for the person who controls it– for example, to post a certain thing, write a specific comment, even to respond automatically to trigger words. If you have the skills, you can also control large numbers of them simultaneously – this is known as a botnet.

This is a vital tool in the scammer's arsenal because imagine the damage you can do with a few thousand bot accounts in your control. You can use them to comment and like a certain post, taking social media algorithms and abusing them to your advantage, making sure as many people are directed to your scam as humanly possible. You could use them to push a certain agenda or to create a certain feeling among those who see their supposed opinions.

You could even, if you were so inclined, use them to buy fake influence. Influence online has become a very marketable currency – if you have a large number of followers for your account, this can easily be turned into money. Brands will pay you for sponsored posts advertising their products. Plenty of people who are not traditional celebrities but whose fame came from the online world have gone down this road.

Beyond the legal but morally questionable uses for bots, what if you were running an account entirely designed to scam people – for example, selling a training course in foreign exchange trading or investing in cryptocurrency online? You could certainly make it look incredibly successful and legitimate if it had 500,000 followers and a massive

< 174 >

amount of positive responses to every post it makes, from people all over the world explaining how it changed their lives and how they wish they had signed up sooner.

Therein lies the problem with bot accounts and fake followers – a scammer running such a scheme could very easily pay for a gigantic following and tons of positive engagement on every post. This kind of smoke and mirrors would absolutely make it seem to anyone who didn't know like the scammers were running an incredibly successful training course that made a lot of people rich – a highly tempting proposition to the next potential victim.

The key thing to remember when dealing with what appears to be highly successful or influential accounts on social media is that their following may not be legitimate. It can be bought and as such should not be treated as a sign that they are trustworthy in any sense. Do not let a high follower count or massive amounts of positive engagement dissuade you from checking review sites, searching online for satisfied customers or asking others if they have used the same product or service.

There are also tools out there to check for bot followers – searching something like 'bot account checker' will find them for you, and many are free. You can cut and paste a web address or social media profile into them and they will tell you immediately what proportion of their followers are suspected bots or fakes. If you're dealing with a scammer, it'll likely be well over half.

THE TELLS

Bot account interaction.

< 175 >

RECOVERY SCAMS

Is this the cruellest scam in the entire book? Quite possibly so. The recovery scam is another fairly recent creation, preying on people at their absolute most vulnerable and looking to take them for every penny possible. It also makes use of bot accounts.

Recovery scammers will operate exclusively on social media, setting up accounts that claim expertise in areas like hacking, recovery of stolen funds and the return of stolen accounts. Most of them have absolutely none of this expertise at all. They use bot accounts on social media primed to respond to trigger words and phrases, along the lines of the following, where they are <u>underlined</u>:

'Can't believe it. My <u>account got hacked</u> last night …'

'Unfortunately, <u>I've been scammed</u> by someone pretending to be my bank …'

'Someone <u>stole my cryptocurrency</u>, I don't even understand how it happened …'

'<u>Lost access</u> to my account. Infuriating!'

'Was talking to him for ages, turned out <u>it was a scam</u> …'

Posting anything like the above sentences on social media due to sheer frustration will doubtless see you receive at least tens of responses from complete strangers who are seemingly sympathizing with your situation. But they aren't just sympathizing; they also have a potential solution to offer you. They will advise that when the same thing happened to them, they contacted an individual called @MrRecoveryScammerOfficial (obviously I've made that name up!) and that this person fixed everything.

These are bot accounts being used by the recovery scammer to drive potential victim traffic their way – they are in effect the scammer's form of advertising. Should you do as they say and contact @MrRecoveryScammerOfficial, you'll be asked to detail what happened and almost certainly to provide some evidence as well. They will claim

< 176 >

that they can help return your account or recover your stolen funds or whatever your problem may be.

In fact, they will do nothing of the sort – it will quickly become clear that in order to help you, they want to be paid. They will likely quote a flat price, which will then creep up as they claim they need to pay for a certain piece of software or crack a certain code and it's harder than they thought it would be. They will also use all the scammer tactics we've previously mentioned in this book to try to take you even further outside your rational mind, when you're still in a panic from already being scammed or having an account hacked: think pressure, impression of urgency, shame and blame.

All their claims are total nonsense; they aren't doing anything apart from extorting you for more money in your time of need. The recovery scammer may even send you images of what they claim is their work on the computer, usually along the lines of typical 'hacker' imagery from films. Think green text on a black background that appears to be in a computer language you don't understand.

Should you comply with their requests for money (inevitably paying by cryptocurrency or similar), they will just keep going and going until you realize it's a scam. It's basic extortion and, unfortunately, it goes after some of the most vulnerable people on the internet – those who have just been scammed.

< 177 >

THE TELLS

Pressure, impression of urgency.

Shame and blame (making you feel embarrassed
or ashamed of your actions).

Unusual payment methods (gift cards, cryptocurrency,
international or bank transfer).

Informational advantage abuse (claiming to
know something you cannot verify).

Bot account interaction.

THE FRUSTRATED POST SCAM

Posting our frustrations and annoyances to social media is a daily fact of life for many, and that's no different when it comes to expressing disappointment at your failure to obtain those extremely in-demand tickets, missing out on the flat you really wanted to rent or anything else that has left you feeling rather frustrated.

In posting about your missing out, you are opening yourself up to a world of pain. As ever, scammers are right on the pulse of what's hot and what's not, whether that's cities where renting property is a serious uphill struggle due to lack of supply, or events that are selling out the world over. They are always thinking of ways they can capitalize on this, and having bots that automatically respond to frustrated posts is one of them.

As with the recovery scams described in the previous segment, the

< 178 >

bots will be keyed up to respond to certain trigger phrases. A good recent example would be Taylor Swift's Eras tour, one of the biggest musical events in the past decade. Tickets across the world sold out in record time, leaving frustrated fans everywhere. The scammer bots were out in force on social media, responding to posted phrases like: 'So sad <u>I missed out on tickets for Eras</u>', 'Absolutely gutted I <u>didn't get tickets to see Taylor</u>' and similar.

Their responses claim to be able to help out – always suggesting they have exactly what you're looking for at a price you'd be willing to pay, or pointing you towards another profile who does, that of the scammer. Much like the duplicated post/Facebook Marketplace scam, however, these scammers will do anything to part a desperate fan – or person in need of an apartment or the latest electrical – with their money, even though they don't actually have the goods in exchange.

They will almost certainly have something set up to demonstrate that the item they claim to have actually exists. If it's tickets, it might be what appears to be a photo of the tickets themselves or a screengrab of the email confirmation – these will, of course, be faked. The scammer will also want payment upfront or a deposit before sending the item or allowing you to see it in person.

Bot accounts that respond to your posts will almost never have the ability to follow up either, so if you are unsure if you're receiving comments from bots trying to direct you to scammers, engage with them. Ask them how they found your post, or if they have previously bought tickets or items from the person they are recommending. The likelihood of the bot formulating a response other than simply posting their original message again is very slim.

< 179 >

THE TELLS

Bot account interaction.

Excuses, excuses (you can't see the item you're buying for some reason).

Unusual payment methods (gift cards, cryptocurrency, international or bank transfer).

CUSTOMER SUPPORT SCAMS

Yet another way in which bots are used for evil purposes on social media, the customer support scam seems to be increasingly popular. It takes the trend for complaining about customer service issues on social media platforms (delayed flights, cancelled trains etc.) and turns it to the scammer's advantage.

Many of us use our social media accounts as a way of holding corporations to account and publicly shaming them for their failings. It's one of the ways in which social media has actually been a force for good, making it much harder for major companies to completely ignore complaints, especially if they gain momentum on social media and end up being picked up by the wider press.

Scammers have seen this behaviour and spotted a weakness. What if they pose as customer service representatives of major brands, setting up accounts that copy the biographies and logos of the brands themselves, and even have handles (names for their accounts) that are very similar to the real thing? In doing so, they are making it possible for the original complainant to mistake them

< 180 >

for a genuine customer service representative of the company they are calling out.

It works like this: the scammer replies to the original complaint (let's say it was about 'StapleAir' cancelling a flight and failing to offer a same-day replacement). The scammer's account is called something like @StapleAirOfficialCustomerSupport and responds in exactly the way a genuine customer service representative, working for the genuine organization, would: 'Sorry to hear about your experience. Can you get in touch via Direct Message and we'll look into this for you. Thanks, Jane'.

Seeing the reply from what appears to be the official customer support, the original complainant replies by direct message, which is a user-to-user message, not publicly visible. At this point, the scammer begins requesting personal information, such as their reservation number and the name on the account. They will explain a refund process similar to what was explained in the Online Shopping Scam segment earlier in the book. This will end up with the original complainant defrauded for the cost of their flights or trains rather than being refunded for it.

The only way you can protect yourself against this is to be absolutely sure you're dealing with the genuine page of StapleAir before replying. You can check by using a search engine to find the company's official website and looking for their social media links there, usually represented by the logo of the social media company you want. Click through and you will be on their official page, which is likely to be something simple like '@StapleAir' and run by multiple employees. Only that account should be trusted to help you with your issue – failing that, contact the company by more traditional customer support means, like over the phone, again taking the number from their official site.

< 181 >

THE TELLS

Dodgy URL (in this case not a web address, but a social media handle that isn't the official account as it claims).

Unusual actions (moving around large amounts of money, sharing one-time passcodes).

Unusual payment methods (gift cards, cryptocurrency, international or bank transfer).

Requests for excessive personal information.

GHOST BROKERS

Social media is, generally speaking, a bad place to shop for or accidentally discover people who claim to provide hugely important services and products like car or home insurance. This scam often originates with an advert or recommendation on social media, and the resulting consequences can be very serious indeed. It's probably the only scam in the book that can potentially result in you, the victim, going to prison.

Ghost brokers are scammers who advertise their skills as insurance brokers. Some will advertise on social media, in posts on local interest groups and pages, others will work by word of mouth. What they promise is to be able to get excellent deals for their customers on insurance products for their cars, houses and valuables.

The scammer posing as a broker will take all of your information just as a genuine broker will, but through methods they won't be able or will refuse to explain to you, achieve a staggeringly cheap price compared to whatever else you're being offered. To pull it off, they

< 182 >

will do one of a few things, all of which will have dire consequences for you personally.

They might adjust your details before sending them on to genuine insurance companies, maybe by giving you more years' experience driving if it's a car, or by lying about the estimated value of the property if it's a house. Either way, when you come to need it, your insurance won't be valid and you'll not be able to make a claim.

Another, even more terrifying possibility is that they take your details, charge you for their services and the cost of insurance but then send you a doctored or manipulated cover letter and insurance documents. This will leave you driving around uninsured, believing that you have paid and are covered – but the responsibility for that lies with you. The ghost broker never took out any genuine insurance for you at all.

The last method a ghost broker might use will be to take your details, alter them slightly and set up genuine insurance at a cheaper price than you'd be able to get by being honest. They will send you real documents, charge you for the insurance (plus their fee) but cancel it immediately after without telling you, taking the refund. Again, this will leave you uninsured when you believe you're covered. All this could result in disastrous consequences: for example, if it were car insurance and you were involved in an accident, you could face jail time. The other person involved in the crash would have no recourse at all, as you were uninsured.

You can protect yourself against these frauds, in the UK at least, by checking any broker you do use on the Financial Conduct Authority (FCA) website or the British Insurance Brokers' Association register. If they're not listed there, think long and hard before going ahead with whatever they are offering. Other nations will have similar authorities or agencies, so check yours. It's also worth bearing in mind a lesson that applies to shopping around for anything, from a builder to work on your home to a new computer: if there is one place or person offering whatever you need at a considerably cheaper price than their competitors,

< 183 >

ask yourself why. In all likelihood, it's a scam. Products and services do tend to have intrinsic value, so one suddenly being miles apart from the others should be a huge red flag.

THE TELLS

The lure (an attractive offer to tempt you – in this case, a cheaper price than anyone else can offer for insurance).

Informational advantage abuse (claiming to know something you cannot verify).

TAX ASSISTANCE AND REBATE SCAMS

Of the same ilk as ghost broking, companies offering to help with accountancy, your taxes or obtaining rebates on social media or elsewhere online are to be treated with extreme caution. The most common way this results in a scam is an advert on social media that would offer help with a genuine problem – for example, claiming underpaid state pension. It may relate to an issue that has recently been discussed by government, with a proposal to fix the error and see the funds paid to those who are owed them.

The companies behind these adverts will offer to take on the task of reclaiming your underpaid pension or overpaid tax for a small fee. If you click through on one of their ads, you'll be taken to their site to fill out extensive personal information about who you are, your personal affairs that affect tax, like whether you are married, all things that a company assisting in this matter will genuinely need to know. You

< 184 >

will probably be asked to submit photo ID at some stage as well. Once this process is complete, you will likely be returned a form by them by email, which you will need to sign and send back.

This is the crucial stage, however. If you sign this form, you are unwittingly sending over the entire right to run all of your tax affairs to this business – that means they will run everything on your behalf. More unscrupulous operators will use this permission to do things like claim future rebates and keep them. Should you question this, they will likely send you a small portion of the rebate you were due, citing the rest is kept as their 'fee'. Overall, it is unlikely you will see anything like the money you originally expected you might be due when you clicked on the advert – these companies will just charge obscene fees, which almost entirely wipe out whatever they may (legitimately) be able to claim back from the tax man or the Department for Work and Pensions.

The crucial thing to remember is this: you could probably have done all this quite easily yourself, and you would not have had to pay for the privilege at all. Even if you would like to appoint an accountant to check it all for you, do your research first. A simple search engine check of the names of some of the dodgier companies offering this kind of service, alongside the word 'scam', will tell you everything you need to know.

THE TELLS

The lure (an attractive offer to tempt you – in
this case, money you're genuinely due).

< 185 >

A QUICK GUIDE TO ROMANCE SCAM TACTICS

I've spent a good amount of time discussing romance scams, their similarity to pig butchering scams and those who carry out this practice already in Chapter 3, so here I will break down the specific tactics used by romance scammers and how they work. I would hope by this point you will have a good handle on the broad structure of romance scams and their process. It is worth reiterating that pretty much all romance scammers, whether a straight romance scam or one which will pivot into pig butchering, use either an unsolicited approach on social media or a solicited approach on an online dating app or website as a starting point.

Like everyone, I get unsolicited messages on social media all the time. Because of what I do for a living, I like to talk to these people and see what I can find out about how they work, what new tricks they may or may not have. Equally, keeping them talking means that sometimes they will slip up, as one romance scammer did when she accidentally cut and pasted her entire script to me instead of just a single answer.

That's right, romance scammers have scripts – not all of them, but many do. Entire documents (this one was 6,000 words long), written up by their bosses and containing answers to every single question their potential victim could possibly have, as well as backstory, giving their imaginary character real depth. These excerpts from her script reveal an interesting insight into exactly how her employers want her to behave and will help us to investigate the specific tactics used and why it is that they work.

Tactic 1 – Seeding

The most important tactic in the arsenal of any romance scammer is 'seeding'. This is laying the groundwork in the early parts of a new relationship for the requests for money that follow later. The example

< 186 >

of seeding below is taken from the early stages of the romance scammer script accidentally sent to me. Each question is intended to be something that the victim might ask, and the answer the response the scammer must then use.

> Q: *Would you ever spend funds on assisting your partner when in need or in trouble?*
> A: *Of course, I would help in any way possible.*

Why is this effective seeding? Because it plants the idea in the mind of the victim early on that the person they are speaking to would help them out in times of financial hardship. What this then creates for the scammer is the opportunity to frame any requests for money in that same context – for example, by asking why you won't help them out when they stated from the start that is something they would do for a romantic interest. This also allows them to exploit your human nature – the desire to be seen as a good person. Should you not pay, in this context they can frame you as a bad person, thanks to the seeding of this concept right at the start of the relationship.

Tactic 2 – Love-bombing

It is difficult to use a specific example from the script to demonstrate this tactic, but it's fairly self-explanatory. In the first weeks of the new relationship, the romance scammer will inundate their potential victim with messages. Contact won't be just daily, it will be hourly, even minute-to-minute, to make the victim feel like there is a real connection with this new person.

In the exciting first days of a new relationship, this is exactly what you want, especially if you are lonely or have been unwillingly single for a long time. A seemingly instant connection, where you find yourself on

< 187 >

the receiving end of a limitless wave of compliments. Inevitably, it feels very good indeed.

The romance scammer's intent here is to start to make you feel reliant on them to feel good. It can even be overwhelming for the victim, who might feel like the relationship is moving too fast. The scammer will know this and won't have any problem throwing extreme declarations of love out there very quickly indeed. This creates a kind of false intimacy, with the victim made to feel very close to the scammer from the start. The scammer knows that once this bond is established, they can begin abusing it. This leads to the following tactics …

Tactic 3 – Isolation

The isolation of their victim from sources of support is romance scammer 101. Having seeded early the ideas that they will call back to later, the scammer will attempt to make the victim feel that they cannot discuss the relationship with anyone else. To do this, they might seed ideas early on, like the scammer themselves not having anyone to talk to for support:

Q: Have you talked about your feelings with someone else?
A: Not since I lost my late boyfriend. He was my only confidant. Now I'm trying to find that person that I can talk to again about anything and feel comfortable and safe.

This sense of their solitude in dealing with issues is intended in the same way as a bank impersonation scammer telling you that the investigation you are helping with could be put at risk if you tell anyone about it. The sole purpose here is to make you feel that you can trust them and them alone, and that as they will not have anyone to talk to about your relationship, you should not talk to anyone either. This can then be abused further, should you try to bring up the idea of sharing your

< 188 >

relationship with family members or friends – the scammer will insist that this demonstrates a lack of trust in them on your part and that you do not love them as they love you.

Tactic 4 – Call Backs

The call back is the scammer's key tool in ensuring you pay out when they want you to pay out. Initially set up with seeded ideas early in the conversation, the scammer will literally 'call back' to them as justification for their financial pleas for help. A good example of this drawn from the seeding above is:

Q: Why should I send you money?
A: You know I would do this for you in your time of need, my darling.

It is much harder for the victim to question this action without being made to feel like a bad person in this context. Other call backs which are commonly used by romance scammers include the use of reference to dangerous work. They will seed their physically dangerous profession early, then use it as a justification to request financial assistance when injured at work, as below:

Q: Why do you need my help, you're well paid?
A: You know my job, these things happen a lot when we are welding underwater. I am at the hospital without my wallet, it is back at the oil rig. My arm is broken – please.

This same logic can be applied to other seeded ideas, like children from a previous relationship with rare illnesses, anything which can be successfully used to call back on and weaponize the victim's guilt at potentially not 'being there' for the person they believe is their romantic partner.

< 189 >

Tactic 5 – Unavailability

Another psychological trick employed by the romance scammer, this will usually be related to their line of work, giving them a reason why it is not possible for them to have in-person contact with the victim, nor to have video calls.

Classic examples of this will be that the romance scammer works in the military or that they are at sea, or simply in areas of very poor reception on a regular basis. This works in their favour as they are using an entirely fake profile to talk to their victim, the pictures are not their real appearance and it is also very likely that their voice does not match their supposed identity. They will always use the justification of their work to avoid video calls or phone calls for these reasons:

Q: It's been so long, I just want to hear your voice. When can we talk?
A: I want to hear your voice so much also, my darling, but before I am back it is impossible for me, dear – the reception is no good.

Beyond this, the unavailability has a psychological effect on the victim, which may well be to make them want their new romantic interest more. It is the romance scammer's version of 'playing hard to get', making themselves unavailable to this person who has come to rely on them to feel good about themselves. This unavailability, in the short term at least, can only serve to strengthen the bond between the romance scammer and their victim – we humans always want what we can't have.

If you find yourself talking to someone online and feel that they are engaging in any of the practices outlined above, please try to remove yourself from the relationship as soon as you possibly can. You are definitely talking to a scammer.

< 190 >

7

Postal Scams

Did this letter or flyer come out of the blue?

Assume it's a scam until proven otherwise.

Does it appear to come from a legitimate source?

Can you find the company/organization online or in a local directory? Do they have the bona fides you'd expect – e.g. customer reviews, physical address, company number?

Is there a lure?

For example, being offered a prize/incentive or services at a reduced cost.

Is the letter specifically addressed to you?

Mass mailouts or flyers should be viewed as possible scams until proven otherwise. Even if the letter contains your name, this should not necessarily be viewed as a sign of legitimacy.

Thoroughly verify all the information in the letter before engaging with it. Check and double-check everything that is being offered or explained before committing. Verify the organization using the process above, but also research the offer/product itself by going online or looking in trusted local directories for information.

< 191 >

THE 'LOCAL TRADESMAN' FLYER SCAM

This unbelievably nasty scam has been going on in the UK for decades and unfortunately, given the nature of the scam and the advertised discounts for OAPs it always offers, is very much targeted at pensioners. And where scams work in one country they inevitably spread elsewhere, so this scam will doubtless be occurring across the world.

Scammers posing as local tradesmen will post flyers around well-to-do areas. The flyers will appear to offer the services of a local business with a very generic name, almost always along the lines of driveway repair, roofing, tree surgery or similar. In fact, any trade that can be done with no expectation of qualifications being shown, because the people behind this scam don't have any.

On the flyers will be consumer-friendly phrases like 'fourteen-day cooling-off period', 'OAP discounts of 15 per cent' and 'family business', all designed to be reassuring and to give you confidence in calling them. They will also list a local address for the business and a local landline number to call. Should you research the address online, you will find that no such business exists there and they will make it deliberately difficult to locate by making the address quite vague anyway. The number will also be a dead end when researched, likely a spoofed landline that goes through to a burner mobile, bought to run the scam and then discarded.

Should you call the number and request some work be done, this is what happens: on the day you have made the appointment, a group of men (at least three or four, possibly more) will turn up to do the work. One will enter your home or garden to assess the work and provide a highly competitive quote for whatever is necessary. They will offer discounts for paying in cash.

You allow work to begin and the men will do it, but incredibly badly. They are not skilled tradespeople. At some stage during the job, they

< 192 >

will discover a problem, or generate one themselves while you aren't looking, which will result in the cost of the job escalating massively.

The 'boss' who originally quoted will explain this to you and give you the new price, which will be at least five times what was originally quoted. If you express shock or disappointment, or say that you cannot afford it, you will simply be pressured into paying up. If you don't have the cash in your home to support the payment, you will be encouraged to go to the bank and get it. The boss may even offer to take you himself.

During this discussion, it is not unlikely that one of the boss's colleagues will have used the distraction to burgle your house, sneaking upstairs or into parts of the home that are unoccupied while you're locked in a conversation about pricing. Should you try to refuse to pay the boss, the men will simply intimidate you by implying that they will do damage to your property or violence against you personally, so you pay as much as you possibly can before they leave.

The work they have completed will at best be substandard, at worst downright damaging and unnecessary. On top of that, you will have overpaid to the point of ridiculousness and possibly even been robbed in the process. When you attempt to track down the culprits or report them to the police, the only lead being the flyer, all the information will go nowhere.

THE TELLS

Out-of-the-blue approach.

Excessively cheap initial quote in comparison to other options.

Murky business details.

< 193 >

THE LUCKY WINNER

There will be a lot of crossover in this section with the email scams section, but there are still some scammers who prefer to do things the old-fashioned way. The reasons for this may be because they think it is more likely to achieve results with their target demographic, which for this type of scam does unfortunately tend to be older members of the population.

This scam is very simple, involving the arrival of a letter claiming to show that the recipient is the lucky winner of some kind of prize. It will possibly be addressed to you personally, but it may also be addressed to 'the homeowner' or 'the occupant'. In order to claim whatever prize it is they say you have won, you will be required either to fill out a form that is enclosed with pre-paid postage for return, or to make a phone call.

In essence, this is just an information-gathering exercise designed to part you with data at very low cost to the scammers. What they obtain in getting your information from the imagined prize is certainly more valuable than what they've spent on sending it out. That data can then be used to scam you in a variety of ways. They may also cheekily add a small fee to cover the administration cost of the imaginary prize, which they say can be paid in cash in the return envelope. This will also add to their illicit earnings.

The prize doesn't exist, and the supposed company behind it doesn't either.

< 194 >

THE TELLS

The lure (an attractive offer to tempt you).

Advance fee (a small upfront payment to secure a future benefit, e.g. money).

Murky business details.

THE PSYCHIC SCAM

Regardless whether you believe the world of psychics and mysticism to be bogus or not, this scam absolutely is. It will begin with a letter or postcard through your door which contains the details of a supposedly local psychic and some enticing information. This might be something specific, like the possibility of an exciting event in your future related to love or money, which this psychic has supposedly foreseen. Whatever it is will be intriguing enough that you might be tempted to find out more. However, this psychic has no plan on revealing anything to you without being paid first. This is how their scam works: they will offer you titbits of information in return for money, just enough to keep you interested but never anything specific enough or clear enough to have any real value.

The reality is that the original letter was sent to hundreds, even thousands, of people at the same time, all of whom would be taken down the same path if they respond to it.

< 195 >

THE TELLS

Out-of-the-blue approach.

The lure (an attractive offer to tempt you).

Advance fee (a small upfront payment to
secure a future benefit, e.g. money).

Informational advantage abuse (claiming to
know something you cannot verify).

THE MULTI-LEVEL MARKETING SCAM

This scam could easily have fit into the next chapter of the book, covering in-person scams, but it starts as commonly by post as it does by word of mouth. The idea behind multi-level marketing is quite complicated, and there are certainly legitimate versions of this practice out there. Unfortunately, there are also many which are scams, and this example will be very much the latter.

Part of the reason multi-level marketing schemes (MLMs) have a problematic reputation is the shape of their structure, which is very much a pyramid, connecting them with the notorious Ponzi schemes that defraud large numbers of people. This is, again, not to say that all MLMs are pyramid schemes, some are perfectly legitimate (hello litigious MLM scheme lawyers!), it's just that some of them do operate in this way.

Broadly speaking, the scam MLM scheme will work like this. You receive a letter offering you the chance to make money working for yourself, as part of a larger organization which likely has a long

< 196 >

history of relative financial success. The letter explains that should you sign up, you will be an individual, self-employed but working as a part of thousands of others like you who do the same. It will likely use attractive phrases related to the lifestyle you could have and the financial independence you could be enjoying as an 'independent distributor' of the company's products.

To be able to do the work, once signed up you will be sent whatever product it is that the MLM company sells, which can be anything from dietary supplements to cosmetics, to clothes. Once you receive these products, your job will be to sell these items but also, crucially, to recruit others to do the same. Your commission from selling the products will be one income stream, your commission from recruiting new members will be the other. In theory, you should be able to make good money.

In a scam MLM, this will be impossible. A US-based report on MLMs found that out of thirty companies running MLMs, 99.6 per cent of those working for them actually lost money rather than gained it. This is because of the pyramid structure: the higher you are in the pyramid, the more you are able to make in commission; the lower you are, the more of your pay goes up instead of to you.

When you take into account your expenses, like buying the actual products and being out trying to sell them or sell the idea of selling the products to others to get your own 'downline' sellers (people below you whose commissions help pay you), it becomes very hard indeed, if not impossible, to stay in the black. Meanwhile, those above you, particularly the individual at the very top, make excellent money from the work of the self-employed hundreds or thousands of people below.

THE TELLS

Pyramid/Ponzi structure.

Murky business details.

Informational advantage abuse (claiming to know something you cannot verify).

Out-of-the-blue approach (if recruited by post).

< 198 >

8

In-person Scams

Did this visitor come out of the blue?

Assume it's a scam until proven otherwise. Do not be scared to ask them to leave or to call the police if they are making you feel at all uncomfortable.

Are they offering to do work or claiming it is necessary?

Many doorstep scams begin with an innocent approach from a tradesperson claiming they are 'working in the area' and spotted something on your property that needs attention. Get a second opinion before committing to anything.

Do you feel under pressure?

Pressure selling or making you feel that you must make a decision in a short time is a sure sign that the visitor is attempting to scam you.

Are they asking for money upfront?

Any requests for payment upfront from an unexpected visitor should be viewed with extreme caution, as you have no guarantees they won't simply take the money and leave.

Have you ensured that the visitor's organization is legitimate?

Check what credentials they can show you, such as a company ID. Also check if the organization has a website, a physical address or a company number you can use to verify them.

< 199 >

THE CHARITY COLLECTION SCAM

In the UK, with apologies to the people of the fine city of Nottingham, you may have heard this scam referred to as 'Nottingham Knockers', although in some areas that more specifically refers to pushy young men trying to sell household goods door-to-door at incredibly inflated prices.

This particular scam is more crafty than that, as it uses the incredibly human desire to be seen as charitable and generous against us. This will always begin with a knock at the door from a friendly young stranger, who will claim to be collecting for charity. They may have a bucket to collect cash in, even a piece of paper supposedly spelling out who they are collecting on behalf of. And they will undoubtedly have a decent spiel to give you about the supposed charity, how it benefits people and why it is a worthy cause.

All this sounds perfectly reasonable until you realize the charity doesn't exist. The people knocking on your door are actually just running a theft-by-deception operation on a fairly large scale, hoping their chat on the doorstep will be sufficient to part a large number of people with their money. They will employ classic scam tactics like pressure and shame to try to get you to pay as well, if you don't cough up immediately.

Being able to decipher a real charity collection from a fake one is pretty easy. First of all, anyone collecting for a genuine charity should have photo ID that they can show on the doorstep and proof that they are an employee or working for the charity they claim to be collecting on behalf of. On top of that, they should be able to show you a charity number – real collectors will have this on a document in their possession or it will be on their ID itself. If the visitor is missing any of that, don't be afraid to simply give them a firm 'no' and close the door. If they try to stick around, threaten them with the police.

< 200 >

THE TELLS

Out-of-the-blue approach.

Pressure, impression of urgency.

Shame and blame (making you feel embarrassed
or ashamed of your actions).

THE 'JUST WORKING IN THE AREA' SCAM

This is an absolutely classic scam used by unscrupulous tradespeople the world over and is as simple as a quick word of supposed advice. You will get a knock on your door out of the blue, from a friendly tradesman claiming to be working nearby. They will explain that they just happened to be driving past and noticed something about your property that needs attention. This will obviously be an issue they claim is visible to them from outdoors and will most likely relate to your roof, guttering, porch, windows or brickwork.

They will offer to help you out with it, as they are working nearby, explaining that they are due to finish on the other job soon and can attend to yours. Should you agree and let them start work, they will be doing an almost certainly completely unnecessary job, probably substandard work and most likely overcharging you massively for it. If they are feeling extra cheeky, they might even ask for a deposit to book the work in and then simply never return.

To avoid going down this road, first of all do not accept unsolicited offers from tradespeople on your doorstep. Do your research, get at least one more tradesperson's opinion on the supposed problem with your

< 201 >

property before progressing to any work. You may find that there is nothing wrong at all. When researching tradespeople, ask to speak to previous customers of theirs in the area – if they can't put you in touch with any, it probably means that if they exist, they aren't happy!

THE TELLS

Out-of-the-blue approach.

Pressure, impression of urgency.

Informational advantage abuse (claiming to know something you cannot verify).

Advance fee (a small upfront payment to secure a future benefit, in this case work that may never be completed).

THE LIMITED-TIME-OFFER SCAM

This scam is a classic of the old-school door knocking variety, where salespeople will be sent out by somewhat unscrupulous businesses, looking for potential clients. The basic form of the scam is this – lucky you, person who opens the door, we're running a promotion in your area.

The companies who run these types of scams almost always tend to work within the home improvement sector – we're talking doors and windows, home security, driveways, guttering and the like. The friendly and possibly young faces they employ to do this part of the job will be smartly dressed, carrying all the right documentation and identification,

< 202 >

but the trick they're about to try to pull makes them no better than any other scammer.

Should you let the salesperson in, they may explain that their business is currently running a sort of postcode lottery-type promotion, where certain areas are offered big discounts, but only for a short period – these prices won't be available next week, as the offer will move on to another area. Using this method, they will try to talk you into spending big on whatever home improvement they're selling.

If you're trying to take pause and aren't convinced, they will have various tactics up their sleeve to up the ante. These kinds of home improvements are major purchases, often valued in the thousands, so you shouldn't be rushed into making a decision, but that's exactly what the salesperson will try to do. One of the most classic tactics here is the 'phone call to the manager' to try to get you an even better price. This might result in another seemingly large reduction on top of what you have already been offered with the supposed initial discount.

Ultimately, all this is intended simply to coax you into making a decision you wouldn't otherwise have made, had you been given more time. At the more unscrupulous end of the spectrum, there are salespeople who will also find any excuse possible to stay in your home beyond where you're comfortable, applying the tactics of pressure selling to try to get you over the line beyond the seemingly enormous discounts.

If you repeatedly ask a salesperson to leave, and make clear that you do not want what they are selling, there is no reason at all for them to be there. But cold-calling salespeople using these tactics will unfortunately try every trick in the book, including making you feel uncomfortable by simply not leaving and offering you lines of credit to take out and pay for the work, requiring only a small deposit upfront.

When dealing with a salesperson in your home, the most important question to remember regarding whatever discount they might be offering is: will it still be available next week, when I have had some time to think?

< 203 >

If the answer is ever 'no', you're dealing with a business you don't want to buy anything from. It is highly likely that their prices were comparatively sky-high in the first place, so any discounts are meaningless and whatever work they did might be substandard or use poor-quality products.

THE TELLS

Out-of-the-blue approach.

Pressure, impression of urgency.

THE MARKET RESEARCH SCAM

This scam is extremely basic but functions as an excellent opener for any scammer looking to profile their victims before trying something more extravagant. With apologies to all genuine market research cold-callers out there, it's one of the reasons my advice with cold calls to the door is: don't answer any questions.

A cold-caller, likely with a clipboard and pen, wonders if they can ask you some questions about your behaviour as a consumer. If you think back to Chapter 4 on email scams, this is in essence an in-person version of 'The Prize Winner', without the lure of a prize. You will be asked to give a few personal details, such as your name, email and number, if you're willing.

The questioner will then run through a basic market research questionnaire with you, related to quite mundane activity around shopping or similar. Unfortunately, their real intention is building a profile of you. While you are answering questions, rather than scribbling your answers, they are making notes. Your estimated age. Whether or not

< 204 >

it appears you live alone or with family. The location of security items like key hooks if they are in sight, an alarm system or cameras.

Once they are done with their questionnaire, they will head off, taking with them a decent understanding of your home's security set-up and whether or not they think you are wealthy or vulnerable enough to burgle. Failing that, they will type up their notes and simply sell the profile they have of you on one of the darker corners of the internet, as a form of sucker list.

The key to remember here is that if you're ever asked to answer questions on your doorstep, there is absolutely no harm at all in asking for ID, verification or to be able to check out the company they claim to represent and even contact them before going ahead. If this is genuine market research, none of that will be any problem at all.

THE TELLS

Out-of-the-blue approach.

Requests for excessive personal information.

THE REMOVAL RANSOM SCAM

Moving home is about as stressful and emotionally charged an activity as it's possible to undertake, without doubt up there with the most difficult logistical experiences a lot of us will have to deal with. Unfortunately, as revealed on my podcast *Scam Clinic*, it's also an area that is not very well regulated (in the UK at least), and as such it's a comfortable home for scammers.

< 205 >

The removal ransom scam is exactly as it sounds – a scam in which advantage is taken of the emotional nature of a move and the deep connection we all inevitably have with our belongings. Imagine you've appointed your removalists, who quoted an extremely competitive price, and the day of the move itself comes along. They arrive and collect your possessions in a very swift and professional fashion.

Once out of sight, you are contacted by another employee of the company. There is an issue: this will usually relate either to the weight of your items being higher than expected, them taking up more space than was agreed or similar. If you are moving internationally, the company may try to blame it on a customs issue. Either way, the cost of your quote has suddenly jumped – and it hasn't just risen a bit, it's orders of magnitude higher than was initially quoted, maybe three to five times over what you expected.

You plead your case, explaining that this isn't what was agreed, but the company stick to their guns, and after all, they have your stuff. They may even put you under pressure to pay the increased price within a certain time, explaining that they will not complete the move if you don't.

At this point you are essentially powerless to resist, because you need your things delivered to your new property to be able to continue living your life. You feel that you have no choice but to agree to pay far more than expected. Maybe you leave the company a bad review online or follow up with your local authority (Trading Standards in the UK) or the police, but to the police this is a civil matter and the local authority will not be able to help unless you can prove that the removalists broke the contract. Perhaps they never even made one.

There are a few red flags here, specifically the initially very cheap quote. If it is far below the competitors, this should be viewed as an indicator of a possible scam. On top of that, when engaging in any business that involves taking quotes, always ask to see terms and conditions upfront, as well as to have a contract in place for the work.

< 206 >

THE TELLS

Excessively cheap in comparison to other options.

Pressure, impression of urgency.

THE FAKE QR CODE SCAM

This clever ruse has been doing the rounds for at least a couple of years in the UK and plays on the use of QR codes as a way to access official payment for various products, like parking. For the unaware, QR code stands for 'Quick Response' code, explaining the way in which these images can quickly take you to a certain location online when scanned with your phone's camera. They are essentially a square of smaller black and white squares, a bit like a checkerboard pattern. Once scanned, they automatically offer up a web address you then need to click or tap to navigate to it.

The issue with the use of QR codes in public spaces is how easy it is to fake one. A QR code on a sign can easily be replaced with a sticker that fits perfectly over it, directing the user to an entirely different clone website to take payment for whatever it might be that they are trying to buy. To the naked eye, it will be very difficult to spot, without close inspection, that you are not scanning the original QR code but one that has been added afterwards. Scammers doing this will have a nicely designed clone website behind it to sell the scam, giving you little to no chance of realizing you haven't actually paid for your parking or whatever it may be, you've just paid them. The double effect of this is that if you were paying to use a service, you haven't actually paid for it, opening you up to possible fines and the consequences of not paying them, like court, from the company genuinely offering the service.

< 207 >

The only way to be really sure you aren't dealing with a fake QR code is to check them closely and thoroughly before scanning with your phone's camera and then again check closely the web address you arrive at to pay. Is it actually the correct address for the company you were expecting it to be?

THE TELLS

Dodgy URL (the web address is not the official website of the company it claims to be).

THE FAKE ONLINE BANKING APP

Earlier in the book, I mentioned that we would go into more detail on the dangers of selling in-person from online marketplaces. This scam is one such problem, taking the imagined ease of paying using the UK's brilliantly efficient bank transfer system and turning it against those who want to sell their items in person.

Scammers have found a way to trick us into giving them items for free, with the use of a bit of clever social engineering and an entirely fake online banking application for a smartphone. It works like this ... You are selling a high-value product online and receive interest from a person who offers to pick it up. When they attend to collect the item and pay (incidentally, this scam only works on a site like Facebook Marketplace, where no responsibility is taken by the site for how payments are made), they want to send the money via bank transfer. They inspect whatever you're selling, and use their smartphone to set up the transfer, showing you every stage of the process, including filling in your details and a timestamped confirmation page that the transfer has been made.

< 208 >

The money doesn't arrive immediately, though, as it normally should. You question this, so they offer to check by searching online, where it does appear that these things can take longer. You wait a little for the money to arrive – but no sign, and unfortunately they are in a bit of a rush. Finally, they produce photo ID, which seems to match the social media profile they were using and also shows their home address. They allow you to take a photo and promise that if the money doesn't arrive, at least you know who they are and where they live.

Begrudgingly, you let them leave with your stuff, satisfied that you have enough evidence in the bag to go and get your money if it never turns up. But it doesn't ever turn up. When you go online, the profile they used to contact you is gone or has blocked you. Then, when you study the image of their photo ID more closely, you realize it's a fake too. The entire process was controlled by the scammer throughout, with each step designed to buy your trust a bit further and let them steal your goods by deception. The banking application they showed you was also entirely fake.

It's a very devious scam and one that is very hard to spot. The best protection in this situation is to insist on payment being made through a third party like PayPal, to put the responsibility of the transaction onto a business and not just on you.

THE TELLS

Pressure, impression of urgency.

Dodgy documentation (fake invoices etc.).

Unusual payment methods (bank transfer in this case is not an unusual payment method but a very problematic one for this specific type of transaction).

< 209 >

Part Three

HELPING YOURSELF AND OTHERS

9

You've Been Scammed: What Next?

The worst has happened: you have been scammed and your money is gone. First of all, it might seem like it is, but it's not the end of the world. If you're in the Western world, there are a lot of consumer protections in place that can help you. Depending on the type of scam, your course of action will need to vary, but I'll outline some of the most important things to know and how to act if you find yourself in that difficult situation.

AUTOMATED PUSH PAYMENT FRAUD (APP FRAUD)

This complicated name is what the banking systems call it when a scam victim is socially engineered into sending money voluntarily. In the UK, this will mean sending money out of their bank account in the course of a scam, either by bank transfer, by transacting it over to another account (e.g. a cryptocurrency wallet) or similar. In terms of scams this would apply to, think bank impersonation (a caller tricking you by posing as your bank to defraud you), refund scams, investment scams and the like. It would not include something paid for using a card or a purchase scam, for example.

< 213 >

In the UK – the first country to introduce such protections – recent legislative change has meant that any APP fraud victim should be refunded up to the value of £85,000 (as of October 2024), provided the bank do not believe the victim has been 'unduly negligent'. This amount will be split between the sending and receiving bank and returned to the victim.

Step 1

In this situation, as with almost all scams, the first port of call should be your bank. You can contact them using the number on the back of your debit card, at the top of a paper statement or in the UK by dialling 159 and choosing the correct option on the automated switchboard. Ask to speak to the fraud department and explain as honestly as you can what has happened, from first contact to your moment of realization. Tell them key details as soon as you can, like the account the money was sent to. They will request evidence to support your claim.

Step 2

Talk to someone. Tell a trusted family member or friend what has happened as soon as you can. This may be very difficult given the feelings of shame and embarrassment you may be feeling, but do your best to open up to someone – a problem shared is a problem halved. It's highly likely that they will be supportive and do their best to help you. It will also help to have a second opinion, should the scammer try to contact you again. Try to have some time to pause and take a breath with whoever you choose to talk to before you begin Step 3. (See also Chapter 11: How to Talk About Scams.)

< 214 >

Step 3

Compile your evidence. Write a timeline of events in bullet-point form to make it very easy for anyone who has not seen or heard what happened to understand it. If you have phone numbers, names or any further information like the bank account you sent money to, include these. Your bank may request images of text messages if you have received them. If you don't know how to send these, ask a trusted friend or family member to show you how to do screengrabs. Attach all this information to an email and send it.

Step 4

Wait. Have faith in the system – your bank's fraud department will get back to you with an answer. During this time, you could report the scam to the relevant government department and to the police to obtain a crime reference number, which will almost certainly come in handy. In the UK currently, the national reporting centre for cyber crime and fraud is Action Fraud; in the US, you would report to the Internet Crime Complaint Center or IC3.

Step 5

Hopefully, when your bank respond they will agree to refund you. Should they dispute your claim and attempt to argue that you should not be refunded, you have a further recourse. In order to go down this road you need to make an official complaint, then give your bank their statutory eight weeks to respond to it. At some stage during this response period, they will issue a 'Final Decision' letter. You will need this to take them to the ombudsman.

< 215 >

Step 6

This is the same process you completed with your bank, but this time sending all the information you have to the financial ombudsman. Send over all the evidence you think supports your case and request a full refund. If the ombudsman finds in your favour (decisions can unfortunately take months), they can request the bank refund you in full, or partially. You may also be compensated if the ombudsman believes your bank acted improperly.

PAYMENTS MADE USING CARD OR CASH, PURCHASE SCAMS ETC.

This section applies to any scam where you believe you have paid for something, either by debit or credit card or cash, and it has turned out to be a scam.

Step 1

As in APP Fraud (above), contact your bank's fraud department and ask to speak to someone. Explain the situation and request a refund. If you have paid by credit card, a refund should be possible very quickly, as the bank can simply call back the funds. This is why, provided credit cards are used responsibly, it's always a good idea to make purchases of items online using one.

If you have paid using a third-party payment provider like PayPal, contact their customer services and explain the situation – they may be able to pause or hold the transaction while they investigate.

If the scam occurred on a website geared for buying and selling (unlike Facebook Marketplace, think eBay etc.), it is also worth reporting the scam to them. They will be able to suspend the account that scammed

< 216 >

you, and as they have oversight of the transaction, they can pause it or put it on hold too.

Step 2

Talk to someone, like a trusted friend or family member as per step 2 above, and see also Chapter 11: How to Talk About Scams.

Step 3

Compile evidence as necessary and send to your bank/the payment provider/site where the scam occurred. This can be the original post of the item that did not exist, any images you've been able to make of the process of the transaction, or the website address you purchased from. Anything you have to prove the fraud occurred will help.

Step 4

Depending on the amount lost, you may be able to go to the financial ombudsman, but the starting point in law is that if the customer made or authorized the payment themselves, it is their responsibility. Unlike an APP scam, where there is specific provision in law for you to be refunded, you may struggle to have a decision in your favour. As for APP scams above, report the scam to the police and your local authority, like Action Fraud in the UK.

USEFUL RESOURCES

Below, I have laid out an example of a timeline that I think would be useful to your bank and any other authorities you need to make aware of

< 217 >

a bank impersonation scam that has occurred. Feel free to use this format in reporting any scam and providing evidence, adjusting as necessary. Example timeline:

The Scam

1. On date XX at 12 p.m., I was contacted by phone, by a person calling themselves Mr Scammer. He was calling from the number 01234 567 891.

2. Mr Scammer explained that there had been fraudulent transactions on my account and that I needed to move my money to a safe account while his department of the bank investigated.

3. During the next two hours, Mr Scammer explained that he needed to install an application onto my computer to help me send the money.

4. With his help, I sent money to a Mrs Scammer, believing they were part of the bank's investigation team. The account details were sort code: 01-02-03 and account number 12345678.

5. The money was sent at 2.04 p.m.

6. Shortly afterwards, the call ended and I realized I might have been scammed. I reported the scam to your bank at 2.15 p.m.

Once you are on top of the timeline of events and evidence in this way and they have been sent off, if you are not happy with how your case has been dealt with and wish to make an official complaint to any kind of financial institution including a bank, you'll need to put it in writing. It's up to you whether this is sent as an email or by traditional post,

< 218 >

though if it's the latter make sure it's recorded delivery so you can be sure it arrived.

Whatever you write will need to include your case reference, exactly what the problem is and, crucially, that you are providing the organization with their eight weeks' notice that you may wish to escalate this to the financial ombudsman.

Example complaint in writing:

> I wish to make an official complaint regarding the way my case (provide the case reference number, which your financial institution will have provided) has been dealt with.
>
> On the x of month y, I was scammed. I have provided all evidence I believe necessary to demonstrate what happened and have not received the result I was expecting/received a full refund/am not happy with the service I have received (delete as appropriate). I do not believe I was negligent or at fault. I am the victim of a crime.
>
> This correspondence should be viewed as the statutory eight weeks' notice that I wish to take this case to the financial ombudsman, pending your final response. Please investigate this and issue your final response letter as soon as possible.

As well as the actions you can take yourself, there are plenty of other support networks and organizations out there who may be able to help you. In the UK, Citizens Advice have excellent help pages online to guide you through the practicalities of what to do after a scam. There are also some excellent specialist legal firms out there who can help if you're willing to pay for some professional assistance in recovering your funds after a scam. Just make sure you apply your due diligence to whoever you appoint, reading reviews online and background checking the business thoroughly to avoid those pesky recovery scammers.

< 219 >

10

Reporting Scams

If you have been scammed, reporting the scam is extremely important. It helps not only to form accurate statistics but to build a picture of the wider scale of fraud and to keep the authorities on top of the changing face of the industry and each new scam that is developed. Only 32 per cent of victims of scams in the UK actually do this, which contributes to the massively underestimated official figures we have on what it costs our societies, globally speaking. If everyone who was scammed realized how necessary and important it was to tell the authorities about it, we might well see faster and more aggressive action at government level to try to put a stop to the problem.

The tools for the reporting of scams in the UK at least are regrettably not centralized – there is no single body you can go to and explain that you have been scammed. This may change in the near future, but for the moment the picture of where to go with your scam report is as follows (and please note that all numbers are correct at the time of going to print):

Phone scams

Report to Action Fraud (www.actionfraud.police.uk) or call 0300 123 2040 in England and Wales, in Scotland dial 101.

< 221 >

Email scams

In the UK, the best thing to do is forward the email to the UK government's phishing address: report@phishing.gov.uk

Text scams

Forward to 7726.

To do this, take a note of the sender, tap and hold the message contents. Look for the 'more' option – on an iPhone this is the word itself, whereas on an Android it's represented by three dots. Press 'forward' and send to 7726, including the number or name of the sender with the new message.

Social media/online world scams

If you have clicked through to a page you think is suspicious or wish to report a scam on social media, you need to do so via the National Cybersecurity Centre's website (www.ncsc.gov.uk/section/about-this-website/report-scam-website). To do this, you will need to fill out their form, which is easy enough but will involve copying and pasting the web address of the site/scam profile into their form.

If you have seen an advert on social media which you believe to be a scam, you should report it to the Advertising Standards Agency using the same method and the following address: www.asa.org.uk/make-a-complaint/report-an-online-scam-ad.html

Postal scams

The Royal Mail website's form is the best place to report scam letters received, although you can also contact Action Fraud (see opposite) and report it to them. Royal Mail's website is: www.royalmail.com/reportingscammail

< 222 >

In-person scams

Action Fraud (www.actionfraud.police.uk) is the best place to report any in-person scam attempt. If the scam was being run by a business with a limited company and you have the details, you can also report it to your local Trading Standards office:

Trading Standards postcode checker (www.gov.uk/find-local-trading-standards-office) is a good way of finding out which jurisdiction you should report the scam company to.

Australia

Australia's centralized system for reporting scams is Scamwatch. Scams of any kind can be reported via their website: https://www.scamwatch.gov.au/report-a-scam

USA

In the US, you can use the Internet Crime Complaint Center (IC3) to report online scams of any kind. This can include phone scams, as many scam calls will have been made using the internet. Their website is www.ic3.gov

< 223 >

11

How to Talk About Scams

In my view, this might be the most important chapter in the book. It is because the way that we speak about scams and the victims of scams is completely wrong – it is so wrong that it is damaging both to those who have not yet been on the receiving end of a scam and to those who have.

The most common responses I see to scam victims sharing their stories are: 'How could they be so stupid/gullible?', 'Do people really not know about this stuff?' or 'I would never have fallen for that.' As a society we have moved on completely from the idea that the victims of serious crimes were somehow at fault, even creating a phrase to mark the behaviour as wrong: victim blaming. Yet when it comes to scams, victim blaming is for some reason not just acceptable but entirely common. If I put the same kind of dialogue in the context of a burglary, it sounds ludicrous to any reasonable person:

'Heard you got burgled. What happened?'

'I was asleep in bed and they used a tool through the letterbox to unhook the keys and opened the door. Took everything downstairs without waking us up, loaded it all into our car and drove off.'

'Wow! You were asleep? And you didn't wake up? What's wrong with you? Leaving the keys by the door is incredibly stupid as well.

< 225 >

Sounds like it was your fault – you really should be more careful like me. I've never been burgled.'

That reads as an incredibly cruel and unfeeling response to the traumatic experience of having your home invaded, because it is. The blame for a burglary should of course lie with the burglar. So, why is it so common to hear this kind of dialogue about scams?

Firstly, it only makes those who do fall victim to scams feel shame and embarrassment at their experience, which makes them less likely to engage with material or advice around scams or to talk to those who might be able to help them. The fact that fewer than a third of scam victims report their experience is demonstrative of the profound effect our manner of speaking about them has.

If everyone was comfortable sharing their experiences of being scammed or having close calls, it would be considerably easier to educate us all about the scams themselves: talking about an issue like this openly and sharing information is a huge part of fixing it. The same goes for reporting: if victims feel able to do it, we get a better overall picture of the severity of the problem, which will hopefully result in better and more aggressive action to solve it on a global scale. Removing the stigma that exists around being the victim of a scam is the first part of that process.

Secondly, this victim blaming forges a feeling of superiority among those who haven't yet fallen for a scam, which essentially benefits scammers. It means that the scammers will approach a huge number of people who simply don't believe this issue is serious enough that they need to protect themselves. As I explained at the start of this book, that is simply not true.

There is a very important and very simple thing to remember about the psychology of scams and how we talk about them. Inevitably, by the time you hear about a scam in the news or from a victim directly, you know a scam has occurred. As such, when you digest the victim's

< 226 >

experience, your scam radar is blinking and you are alert to the possible red flags and tells they may have spotted in the process. But you are only so alert because you *know* it's a scam from the start. The victim did not have that privilege when the approach was made to them, they are not reading about it in the news or hearing about it after the fact: they experienced it directly, in the moment. All the skills the scammer uses to take them out of their rational mind, like pressure, shame and blame and informational advantage, were in play too, making it even harder for the victim to spot and process any signs they might be about to be scammed.

If we're going to better protect ourselves against fraud in the future, we have to forget the nonsense idea that scams only happen to the elderly or the vulnerable or those who aren't technologically savvy. I have seen with my own eyes scam victims from age nineteen to ninety, from people who work in bank security to psychiatrists, to company directors. Changing the conversation is a huge part of altering that entirely false belief.

I will reiterate what I wrote at the start of this book: if you have not yet been scammed, you have simply been lucky. Even more likely, you've just never been caught by the right scam at the wrong time, when you were distracted or when the scam itself coincidentally fit into a real event in your life. It will happen, so being on top of the information available and making others feel comfortable sharing their experiences of scams should be your first priority, not belittling those unfortunate enough to be on the receiving end already.

It might make you feel good to say that you've never been caught by a scammer, but when the tables turn, it simply won't help you. Instead, we need to drive a change in the conversation on a national level to reflect the new reality that we are all possible victims. No more complacency, no more victim blaming. Talk about scams the right way with those around you and be part of the solution, not the problem.

< 227 >

I really hope that this book has gone some way not just towards protecting you from scams but towards helping you see that they are here to stay and that the onus is on us to ensure that we all help one another to stay safe. With community action against the scammers and wider education about scams themselves, I believe that the fight against fraud is one we can win. Let's start now!

< 228 >

Further Reading

NIGERIAN PRINCE TO GHANAIAN HUSBAND

'The Nigerian Prince Email and the History of Social Engineering Techniques', Hackernoon, 21 August 2023.

'The Long Shadow of the "Nigerian Prince' Scam', *Wired*, 10 April 2022.

'Letter from Africa: Why Nigeria's Internet Scammers are "Role Models"', BBC, 23 September 2019.

'How that "Nigerian Email Scam" Got Started', NPR, 22 May 2013.

'Why Do So Many Catfishing Scams Come Out of West Africa?', BBC, 14 February 2023.

'What Do We Know About Online Romance Fraud Studies? A Systematic Review of the Empirical Literature (2000–2021)', *Journal of Economic Criminology*, Vol. 2 (December 2023).

'Sakawa Boys: Meet Ghana's Online Romance Scammers', Reuters, 15 August 2023.

'Identity Expression – The Case of "Sakawa" Boys in Ghana', *Human Arenas*, Vol. 6 (2023), pp. 242–63.

'How Online Love Scams Created a Culture: The Power and Influences behind Sakawa', Walker, May 2023.

< 229 >

SOUTH-EAST ASIA – PIG BUTCHERING ETC.

'A Criminal Cancer Spreads in Southeast Asia', United States Institute of Peace, 26 June 2023.

'"Hundreds of Thousands" Trafficked into SE Asia Scam Centres – UN', Reuters, 29 August 2023.

'7 Months Inside an Online Scam Labor Camp', *The New York Times*, 17 December 2023.

'Why the US and China Should Work Together to Solve the Global Scam Crisis', *The Diplomat*, 15 February 2024.

'"Don't You Remember Me?" The Crypto Hell on the Other Side of a Spam Text', Bloomberg, 17 August 2023.

'Meet Cambodia's Cyber Slaves', Al Jazeera, 11 August 2022.

'Unraveling the Pig Butchering Scam (ShaZhuPan)', Global Anti Scam, 18 April 2022.

MISC.

Sim Swap Fraud, NatWest, available at: www.natwest.com/fraud-and-security/fraud-guide/sim-swapping-scams.html

'Oh No, Grandma Has a Computer: How Internet Fraud Will Take the Place of Telemarketing Fraud Targeting the Elderly', *Santa Clara Law Review*, Vol. 42, No. 2 (2002), pp. 659–88.

'The History and Evolution of Fraud', Fraud.com, available at: www.fraud.com/post/the-history-and-evolution-of-fraud

'Online Scam Operations and Trafficking into Forced Criminality in Southeast Asia: Recommendations for a Human Rights Response', United Nations Human Rights, 2023.

< 230 >

'The Top 5 Hot Spots for Fraud Around the World', Feedzai, 8 June 2022.

'Scare and Sell: Here's How an Indian Call Centre Cheated Foreign Computer Owners', *Hindustan Times*, 18 May 2017.

< 231 >

Index

< 234 >

< 236 >

< 238 >

< 239 >